NUMBER 9

THE BEGINNING

NUMBER 9: THE BEGINNING.
by Jack Scorer

First Edition
Kick Books Publishing

Dear Reader,

Have you ever had a dream so big it scared you? A dream that seemed impossible, like trying to catch a star in the sky. That's exactly how Jack Scorer felt when he won a golden ticket to play soccer at England's most famous academy.

This is more than just a story about soccer. It's about leaving everything you know behind to chase your dreams. It's about finding friendship in unexpected places - from quiet dormitory rooms to noisy street corners. It's about learning that sometimes the biggest victories don't come from scoring goals, but from helping others succeed.

Whether you eat, sleep, and breathe soccer or you're just beginning to learn about the beautiful game, I hope Jack's journey inspires you. I hope it shows you that with enough belief, determination, practice, and help from friends, any dream—no matter how big—is possible.

Sometimes the biggest adventures start with the smallest chances. All you need is the courage to take them.

Welcome to Jack's story.

P.S. Remember, in England, they don't call it soccer—it's football! But don't worry if you get confused. Jack did too!

Dedicated to my parents,
who made this all possible.

1

The Golden Ticket

"Dreams are not what you see in your sleep, they are the things that don't let you sleep."

Cristiano Ronaldo

Jack's heart pounds as he places the ball on the penalty spot. The roar of the Kingsdown Academy crowd fades to a distant hum. This is it—the moment that will decide everything. Ten months of blood, sweat, and tears have led to this.

As he takes five steps back, Jack can't help but think about how different things were just a year ago. He was just a eleven-year-old kid from Austin, Texas, with a crazy dream, and now here he stands, about to take the most important shot of his life. One that could make or break his entire future.

The referee blows his whistle. The crowd falls silent, Jack takes a deep breath, runs forward,

and...

Ten months earlier.

The hot Texas sun beats down on Jack as he kicks his ball against the wall for what feels like the millionth time.

Suddenly, he hears his mom's voice. "Jack, hurry up! You've got to see this!" she shouts from the kitchen.

Jack races inside, his loyal dog Jake hot on his heels.

"What's up, Mom?" Jack asks, bouncing on his toes. "I was in the middle of practising my super-cool soccer moves!"

His mom grins and hands him a small, rectangular gift wrapped in shiny red paper. "I got a present for you. "

Jack's eyes light up like fireworks. He tears into the package like a hungry T-Rex.

"Whoa, awesome! Thanks, Mom!" he exclaims, a smile spreading across his face as wide as the Texas sky.

It's a pack of Premier League trading cards. Jack's always been a collector, but this year is extra special. The card company is running a cool competition. Kids can come to England and play for a professional academy for a whole year! And if the academy thinks you're good enough, they might even sign you as a pro afterwards. For soccer mad Jack, this is the stuff dreams are made of. Jack rips open the pack of cards. He'd been saving his allowance for weeks, buying every pack he could, hoping to find that one golden ticket that could change everything. But so far, no luck.

He dashes to his room to check the cards, his hands shaking.

"Come on, come on," he mutters, flipping through them at lightning speed.

Another striker, a goalkeeper, a midfielder... His heart sinks faster than a stone in water. Nothing. Just like all the other packs. With A sigh that could fill the Grand Canyon, Jack flops onto his bed, tossing the cards aside. He stares at his ceiling, plastered with posters of his soccer heroes.

Ronaldo, Messi, and Kane smile down at him, their success as far away as the moon.

A glint catches Jack's eye. Frowning, he sits up. Something shiny and golden, catches his eye from a distance. Jack's breath catches in his throat as he slowly pulls it out. He can't believe his eyes.

It's a golden ticket! *The* golden ticket!

For a moment, Jack stares, his brain refusing to believe what his eyes are seeing. Then…

"Mom! Dad!" he yells, his voice like thunder. "I won! I'm gonna play soccer in England!"

His parents rush into his room, bursting through the door.

"You're pulling our leg," his mom says, gasping for air.

"No joke." Jack grins, holding up the golden ticket like a pirate flaunting the map to buried treasure. "I'm gonna play soccer in England!"

His dad laughs, ruffling Jack's hair. "Football, son. They call it football over there."

"Football, soccer...whatever! I can't wait!" Jack shouts bouncing up and down on his bed like it's a bouncy castle..

Then reality hits him like a tidal wave: England, a whole different country, a professional team. Suddenly, things become realer than a three-dimensional movie.

Jack has only ever played in the park. His parents often try to get him to join a team and make new friends, but Jack's shy and always comes up with excuses to say no. He did try once, though. A trial for a local team a couple of years back. But it ended up being a total disaster. One of the other kids pulled a mean prank on him, embarrassing Jack in front of everyone. The memory of that day still stings like a swarm of angry bees.

In Jack's mind, if he doesn't try, then he can't fail. He can't be embarrassed or hurt again if he can't fail. It's safer that way. But this? This is different. A chance to play real football, to train at a proper academy. It's like all his birthday wishes are coming true at once. Despite his nerves, Jack knows he has to go.

"When do I leave?" Jack asks excitedly rocking back and forward on his bed.

His mom squints her eyes as she checks the info packet that came with the golden ticket. "In two weeks," she exclaims raising an eyebrow. "We've got a lot to get ready, honey."

Two weeks. It seems both forever and no time at all. The days crawl by like snails, but the excitement in the air is palpable. Jack can't wait to step onto that plane and begin his new adventure. Jack's life becomes a whirlwind of packing, learning about England, last-minute preparations, and tons more soccer practice.

"Shirt: check. Shin guards: check... Cleats..." Jack's voice trails off as he picks up his old, beat-up football cleats. The sole is flapping like a fish out of water.

"Mom!" he calls out biting his lip. "I think I need new boots!"

His mom appears in the doorway, followed closely by his dad.

"Oh, Jack." She sighs. "Why didn't you say something earlier? When we first found out that you'd be going to England?" She frowns.

Jack shrugs. "I thought they'd be okay."

His dad joins them, shaking his head when he sees the cleats. "Those have seen better days, champ. We'll have to get you new ones."

Guilt washes over Jack like a tidal wave. He knows money's tight, especially with all the costs of his trip to England.

"Maybe we could just glue them?" he mutters half-heartedly, picking up a glue stick near on his bedside table.

His parents exchange a glance.

"No, son," his dad says firmly. "You're going to be playing at a top academy. You need proper boots."

Jack hugs his dad. "Thanks, Dad."

As the bedroom door closes, Jack can't help but overhear his parents' hushed conversation.

"It's a lot of money," his mom whispers.

"I know," his dad replies. "But this is his chance. We have to give him the best shot we can."

A lump the size of a football tightens in Jack's throat. He knows his parents are sacrificing so much for his dream, and he'll do anything to make them proud.

The next day, his dad presents Jack with a new pair of boots. Bright red with diagonal white lines running down them.

"Wow!" Jack screams, his eyes nearly popping out of his head. "These are the same ones Ronaldo wears! My absolute favourite!"

"I thought you might like them," his dad replies leaning back with a grin.

"Like them? I *love* them! Thank you so much, Dad!" Jack exclaims unable to take his eyes off them.

"Hey, it's not just me," his dad reminds him. "They're from your mom, too!" ruffling Jacks hair.

Suddenly Jack goes quiet. The mood shifts like a storm cloud rolling in. His wide smile collapses into a worried frown.

"Dad," he says, his voice barely above a whisper. "What if I'm not good enough? What if the other kids don't like me? What if I can't do it?" He fidgets with the laces on his new boots.

His dad's smile doesn't fade. Instead, he wraps Jack in a big bear hug. "You can do anything, Jack. I've watched you practice for hours and hours in the yard, from sunrise to sunset. I've seen your talent. Your determination. You need to see it, too."

"Really?" Jack replies raising an eyebrow.

"Of course."

"But how?" Jack asks softly.

"You just need to believe, Jack. As long as you try your best and give everything you've got, then you can't fail."

"And the other kids? If they don't like me?" he asks, bowing his head.

"Who couldn't like you?" his dad playfully replies, ruffling Jack's hair.

"Well, last time I tried to play for a team, they didn't," Jack mumbles.

"That was just one silly kid," his dad says gently. "Forget about him, Jack. That's in the past. You've been given an opportunity of a lifetime. You have the heart, the talent, and the determination. Now get some belief, and you'll be unstoppable."

"Promise?" Jack says, holding out his pinky finger.

"Promise," Dad replies, locking his finger with Jack's.

"Thanks, Dad. And thanks for the boots. I promise I'll take super good care of them."

His dad ruffles his hair one more time. "I know you will, son. Just remember It's not just about being a star—but about shining bright enough to help others shine, too. Now, get some sleep. Big day tomorrow."

Jack drifts off to sleep, his new boots gleaming in the moonlight like treasure. His phone pings. Bleary-eyed, he opens the message—a video from Kingsdown Academy. His heart races like a cheetah as he watches his future teammates pull off impressive moves, their passes precise as lasers and their shots powerful as rockets. The final clip shows a boy his age scoring an incredible goal that would make even Ronaldo jealous.

Jack's nerves start to kick in. These aren't just kids—they're like mini-Ronaldos and pint-sized Messis! One thought bounces around his head like a pinball: *Am I good enough for this?*

2

Welcome To Football Heaven

"Every time I step onto the field,
I prove that dreams can become reality."

Robert Lewandowski

The aeroplane engines roar as Jack presses his face against the small window. Below him, the familiar landscape of Texas shrinks away quickly, transforming into a patchwork quilt of greens and browns. Jack clutches his backpack close. The memory of his mom and his trusty dog Jake's tearful goodbyes at the airport gate flashes through his mind.

"Here we go Jack" his dad declares, as Jack prepares to leave everything he knows behind.

It's thrilling and scary all at once, like standing at the edge of a high diving board, knowing you must jump, but not quite sure if you're ready. Now, it's time for take off. Jack leans back, closing his eyes as the plane surges forward. Leaving the familiar ground behind, he can't help but wonder if this is what it feels like to soar towards your dreams.

"First time flying?" a kind voice asks, cutting through Jack's thoughts.

Jack sees an older woman with grey hair and glasses sitting beside him. Her eyes crinkle at the corners, reminding him of his grandmother back home.

"Yes." He responds, trying to keep his voice steady even as his hands tremble slightly. "I'm going to England to play football."

"How exciting!" the woman exclaims. "My grandson plays football, too. He's at an academy in London."

"Really? That's where I'm going!" Jack exclaims tilting his head slightly. "To an academy in London."

"Well, isn't that something!" She smiles warmly. "Which academy are you off to, dear?"

"Kingsdown Academy," Jack replies proudly.

The woman's face lights up like a Christmas tree. "That's where my Zico is! He's been there for a couple of years now. It was a bit tricky for him at first," she says kindly. "They expect a lot from you there, you know."

Jack feels a familiar wave of anxiety rising within him as he swallows hard. "I've heard," he replies, his voice a soft murmur. He takes a breath, squares his shoulders, and confidently states, "But I'm ready for anything. Football is my life—I think about it every day."

"That's the spirit," the woman replies, patting his arm. "You remind me of my Zico when he first left. So determined!"

As the flight continues, the woman—who introduces herself as Mrs. Bennett—tells Jack all about London. She points out landmarks as they appear below her, her enthusiasm infectious.

"Whoa, everything looks so tiny! What's that?" he asks, pointing down at a tall tower resembling a fancy pencil sticking out of the ground.

"That's Big Ben," she says, laughing at his amazement. "It's one of the most famous clocks in the world."

Jack's gaze shifts, taking in the sprawling city below. "And that big building?"

"That's Buckingham Palace. The King and his family live there."

"What's that?" Jack asks, pointing to a giant wheel resembling a vast carnival ride.

"That big wheel? That's the London Eye. You get a wonderful view of the city from up there."

Then Jack spots something he has only ever seen in magazines and on TV. His heart skips a beat. "Is that...?"

"Yep." The woman smiles, squinting her eyes to look out of the airplane window once more. "That's Wembley Stadium. The biggest stadium in the UK. Over ninety thousand people fill it to watch sports, mostly football. Or soccer to you." She jokes, with a gentle smile.

Jack gapes at the sight before him, trying to imagine the roar of such a massive crowd. "Wow!"

"It's famous for hosting the FA Cup, the oldest football competition in the country," Mrs Bennett continues. "Some of the greatest football matches have been played right there. The Champions League is played there, too. That's where the best teams from all over Europe compete."

Jack's eyes light up, and his imagination runs wild. He can almost hear the crowd chanting and feel the electric atmosphere of a big match.

"Wembley has hosted the biggest international tournaments, too! The European Championship and the World Cup!"

Jack dreams of one day reaching the final, scoring the winning goal, and lifting the trophy high above his head. His family, in the stands, cheering proudly. The thought sends a shiver of excitement down his spine.

"Only the biggest teams in England get a chance to play there," she explains. "You have to go far in the cup competitions just to set foot on that pitch."

"That's where I want to play!" Jack confidently declares.

"Well, that's where the big-league players go. You'll have to work your socks off to get there," Mrs. Bennett says with a kind smile.

Jack grins confidently, his earlier nervousness all but forgotten. "I can do it—I know it!"

As they descend, Mrs. Bennett gives Jack one last piece of advice. "Well, if you need a friendly face at the academy, look for my Zico. He's always happy to help new players."

Jack nods gratefully, feeling a little less alone. "Thanks, I will."

The captain's voice crackles over the intercom. "Ladies and gentlemen, we're beginning our descent into London Heathrow Airport."

Jack's face lights up as the plane makes its descent. Catching a glimpse of the huge airport for the first time.

As soon as Jack steps off the plane, he's hit by the cooler, crisp air and notices it's raining, even though it's summer. The sound of raindrops against the windows is almost musical. He shivers a little as he puts on his raincoat, glad his mom insisted he pack a jacket in his carry-on. The fabric feels comforting, like a hug from home.

Jack and his dad make their way to passport control.

"Welcome to the United Kingdom," a friendly voice says as he approaches passport control.

Jack hands over his documents, trying not to look as nervous as he feels. His palms are sweaty, and he wipes them discreetly on his jeans.

"What is the purpose of your visit?" the officer asks, his accent thick and unfamiliar to Jack's ears.

"I'm here to play football," Jack says proudly.

The officer raises an eyebrow, a small smile playing on his lips. "Are you now? Well, good luck with that, young man."

As he waits for his luggage, Jack can't stop looking around. Everything seems slightly different—the signs, the accents he can hear around him, even the smell of the air. It's exciting and overwhelming, like stepping into a new world. He spots a baggage trolley nearby and places his luggage down. As he walks toward the arrivals section, he wishes he had chosen a less squeaky trolley.

"Jack Scorer?" a voice calls out, cutting through the bustle of the airport.

A man in a tracksuit with the Kingsdown Academy logo is waving at him at arrivals. Jack's heart leaps into his throat. This is it—the real beginning of his adventure.

"Welcome to England! How was the flight? You ready for your big adventure?" the man exclaims gesturing broadly towards Jack.

Jack takes a deep breath. A mix of nervousness and excitement bubbles in his chest, but he manages a confident nod. He's ready.

He gives his dad a huge hug and says his tearful goodbye. Then climbs into the academy van. Jack thinks about his mom and dog back in Texas. He imagines them at home, probably worried sick but proud, too. "I'll make you proud," he whispers as the van pulls away from the curb, the airport shrinking in the rearview mirror.

Jack's new life is about to begin. The road ahead is uncertain, filled with challenges he can't imagine yet. But as he watches the London landscape whiz by, Jack feels a surge of determination. He's determined to make the most of it, no matter what.

This is his shot at becoming a star, and he isn't going to waste it.

3

First Day Fumbles

"The more difficult the victory,
the greater the happiness in winning."

Pelé

The taxi ride is over in a flash. Jack soon finds himself outside the famous Kingsdown Academy gates.

"Here we are, lad," the driver announces. "Kingsdown Academy."

Jack jumps out of the taxi, his eyes full with wonder. Kingsdown is the oldest and most prestigious football academy in the world. It has produced some of the finest players worldwide, winning eighteen of the last twenty league titles.

Jack takes in the scene before him, each detail carving itself into his memory like the design on his favorite ball. The field stretches out like an endless green canvas, promising adventures that no Xbox game can provide. For the first time since leaving Texas, the knot of homesickness in his chest loosens, replaced by a feeling that surprisingly resembles belonging. This isn't just another pitch; it's an invitation for him to prove himself.

Huge red brick buildings that look like castles surround him. He spots statues of his favourite stars on the grass, looking ready to jump into action. The smell of fresh-cut grass tickles his nose, mixed with the leathery scent of new footballs. His ears pick up the familiar sounds of kids laughing, coaches whistling, and the satisfying thump of boots kicking balls. Clutching his new boots, Jack feels excitement and nerves in his stomach. This is it—the place where young players like him come to become champions.

"Jack Scorer?" a tall man with a clipboard calls from a distance.

"Yep, that's me," Jack replies nodding almost uncontrollably.

The man is tall and muscular, with no hair except for a well-groomed mustache. He has a kind face but carries himself with an air of authority. "Welcome to Kingsdown. I'm Coach Wilkinson," he says with a smile. "Let's get you settled in, shall we?" He gestures toward the entrance.

As they walk, Coach Wilkinson points out various buildings and fields. "That's the main training pitch... There's the gym... Those are the dormitories where you'll be staying..."

Jack tries to take it all in, but his head is spinning. Everything looks so new, so professional, so amazing.

"Now, Jack," Coach Wilkinson states as they reach the dormitories. "It's a lot to take in, isn't it?"

Jack gives an eager bob of agreement, shuffling his feet.

"Just remember, every lad here started off just like you," Coach continues. "Give it time, work hard, and you'll fit right in."

Jack nods, grateful for the encouragement.

"Your roommate should be here to show you around," Coach says, checking his watch. "Ah, here he comes now."

A boy about Jack's age jogs towards them. He's small like Jack, with curly brown hair and a friendly grin.

"Jack, this is Tommy"—pointing to scrawny looking pale boy nearby—"He'll be your roommate and guide for the first few days."

Tommy sticks out his hand. "Hey! Welcome to football heaven, or soccer heaven, as you guys say!"

Jack shakes his hand, relieved by Tommy's friendliness. "Thanks. Nice to meet you."

"Right, I'll leave you lads to it," Coach Wilkinson says. "Jack, we'll see you bright and early tomorrow for your first training session. Get some rest."

As Coach walks away, Tommy grabs one of Jack's bags.

"Come on, I'll show you our room. To warn you, it's not exactly a five-star hotel," he jokes.

Jack follows Tommy into the dormitory building. The corridors are a maze of identical white doors, a little like a hospital, minus the sick people that is!. Tommy navigates them with ease. Like he has a built in GPS.

"Here we are," Tommy announces, pushing open the door. "Home sweet home."

The room is small, with two narrow beds, two drawers, two desks, and nothing else. But to Jack, it's perfect. As he unpacks, Jack and Tommy chat. Tommy is from Manchester and has been at the academy for a year. All of his family members have been professional players, and he is next in line.

"So, you're from America, eh?" Tommy asks, quirking an eyebrow. "What's that like?"

Jack shrugs. "It's cool. Bigger, I guess. And hotter, for sure," he adds with a laugh.

Tommy chuckles. "Well, you'll get used to the rain here soon enough."

Just then, there's a knock at the door. A boy with dark, messy hair and a friendly grin pokes his head in.

"New kid's arrived, then?" he barks. "I'm Zico. Team captain."

Jack's jaw drops. "Zico? I met your gran on the plane!"

Zico laughs. "Small world! How was she?"

"She was great," Jack replies. "She showed me Wembley Stadium from the plane."

"Ah, where legends are born," Zico says, smiling.

Jack feels his nerves melt away. "So, what's it like here?"

"It's awesome!" Zico exclaims. "Tough training, but loads of fun too. You'll see tomorrow." Zico glances at his watch.

"Oops, it's getting late. Better let you get some sleep. The first day's always crazy."

"Thanks, Zico," Jack replies, trying to fight back a yawn.

"No worries, mate. Sleep tight!" Zico waves, closing the door softly behind him.

As Jack snuggles into his new bed, he smiles. This place won't be so scary after all.

The following day, a loud noise jolts Jack awake. *Beep! Beep! Beep!*

"Everybody up! The first training of the day!" Coach's voice blasts over the speaker.

"Hey, new kid, wake up! It's time for training!" Tommy calls out.

"Training?" Jack replies, still half-asleep.

"Yes, the very thing you came here for," Tommy jokes.

"Oh, we call it practice in America," Jack explains, rubbing his eyes.

"Well, whatever you call it, we must get moving!" Tommy declares, tossing Jack his training kit.

He puts it on, and they make their way out. Jack freezes when they reach the training ground, gazing at the amazing sight before him. The pitch is perfect, the grass a green carpet stretching out before him. White lines zip across the field like racetracks. With what seems like a million balls scattered everywhere. Jack grins, leaning back. This isn't just a field. This is heaven.

Other boys are already there, warming up and chatting. They seem bigger, stronger, and faster than Jack. The coaches bark orders at the players. It reminds Jack more of an army boot camp than a football academy.

Coach Wilkinson's whistle cuts through the chilly morning air. "Alright, lads! Let's get started. Ten laps around the pitch to warm up."

Jack sets off, clenching his fists, determined to make a good impression. But as the laps go on, he finds himself falling behind. The other boys seem to glide effortlessly while Jack's lungs burn, and his legs feel like stone.

"Keep up, Scorer!" Coach yells. "This is just the warm-up!"

Red-faced and panting, Jack finally finishes his laps. He's last, and the other boys gather around Coach Wilkinson for the following instructions.

"Right, we'll start with some passing drills," Coach announces. "Pair up!"

Jack looks around, hoping to catch Tommy's eye, but his roommate has already partnered with someone else. Everyone seems to have a partner except...

"Looks like it's you and me, American," a voice says. Jack turns to see a tall, muscular boy with long blond hair smirking at him. "I'm Wilson."

Jack quickly realises he's out of his depth as they begin passing the ball back and forth. Wilson's passes are crisp and accurate, while Jack's are often off-target or too weak.

"Come on, Scorer!" Coach Wilkinson calls out. "Sharpen up those passes!"

Jack grits his teeth, trying to focus. But the more he tries, the worse he gets. Wilson's smirk grows wider with each of Jack's mistakes. The rest of the session doesn't go much better either. Jack's first attempt during the shooting drill goes wide of the goal. His second dribbles weakly to the keeper, and his third... Well, the less said about that, the better.

By the end of training, Jack is exhausted, discouraged, and covered in mud from a particularly embarrassing fall during a dribbling exercise. As the other boys head to the showers, Coach Wilkinson calls Jack over.

Coach has his arms crossed. He looks like he means business. "Scorer," he states, his voice serious. "I know it's your first day, but I have to be honest—you're not at the level we expect here at Kingsdown."

Jack's heart sinks. Dropping his chin to his chest. "I'm sorry, Coach. I'll do better, I promise."

"I hope so, lad. Because right now, you've got a lot of work to do if you want to stay here."

As Jack limps back to the dormitory, Wilson calls out behind him, "Hey, Yankee! Try sticking to baseball!"

Laughter echoes across the field as Jack moves faster, fighting back tears. This is far from the dream he had imagined.

Back in his room, Jack sits on his bed, staring at his muddy boots. He thinks of his parents, of the sacrifice they made to buy these boots. He remembers his friends back in Texas and their games at the park. For the first time since arriving in England, Jack wonders if he's made a terrible mistake.

4

Friends And Foes

"In football, as in life, you need both good teammates and worthy opponents to reach your full potential."

Karim Benzema

The weeks following Jack's arrival at Kingsdown Academy fly by in a blur of training sessions and adjusting to life in a new country. Each day brings new challenges but also small victories that make Jack feel like he's slowly finding his place.

One chilly morning, Jack wakes up earlier than usual. He lies in bed, listening to the unfamiliar sounds of the dormitory—the soft snores of his roommate, the distant hum of the heating system, and the patter of rain against the window. It's so different from the sounds of home that a wave of homesickness washed over him.

Quietly, to avoid waking Tommy, Jack slips out of bed and pads to the window. The academy grounds are shrouded in mist, the football fields barely visible. It looks like something out of a movie, so different from the dry, sunny mornings he's used to in Texas.

"Can't sleep?" Tommy's sleepy voice comes from across the room.

Jack turns, surprised. "Sorry, did I wake you?"

Tommy sits up, rubbing his eyes. "Nah, mate, I'm always up early. Dad says the early bird catches the worm."

Jack chuckles. "My dad says that too. I guess dads are the same everywhere."

Tommy grins. "Want to go for a run? We've got an hour before breakfast."

Jack hesitates. He isn't used to running in the rain, but the thought of lying in bed missing home isn't appealing either. "Sure, why not?"

They dress quickly and quietly and head outside. The rain has eased to a light drizzle. The grass is slick under their feet as they jog around the perimeter of the academy.

Tommy points out different buildings as they run and share stories about the academy's history. Jack relaxes, laughing at Tommy's jokes and feeling less like an outsider with each step.

"So," Tommy says as they round a corner, "how are you finding it here? For real?"

Jack stares around the pitch as he considers the question. "It's...different," he says finally. "Everything's so new. The food, the weather, and even the way you guys talk. Sometimes I feel like I'm on another planet."

Tommy nods sympathetically. "I get it. I felt the same way when I first came here from Manchester. London's a whole different world."

"You're not from here either?" Jack asks, blinking rapidly in surprise.

"Nope. Moved down last year. It was tough at first, being away from home."

"Does it get easier?" Jack murmers.

Tommy smiles. "Yeah, it does. You make friends. You get used to the routine. Before you know it, it starts feeling like home."

As they complete their lap, the sun breaks through the clouds, casting a golden glow over the misty fields.

"Race you to breakfast?" Tommy challenges.

Jack looks him directly in the eyes and says, "You're on!"

They take off, their laughter echoing across the grounds. As Jack runs, he feels something shift inside him. For the first time since arriving, he feels happy. *Maybe*, he thought, *Tommy's right. Maybe this place can become home.*

Over the next few weeks, Jack and Tommy fall into a routine. They wake up early for runs, talk about football, and stay late after training to practice. Jack finds himself improving rapidly, both on and off the field.

One evening, after a particularly grueling training session, Tommy turns to Jack, rubbing the back of his neck and wearing a serious expression.

"You know, I'm glad you're here," he states. "It's nice having a friend who gets it, you know?"

Jack nods, touched by Tommy's words. "Me too. I don't know if I could've stuck it out here without you."

Tommy places his hand on Jacks shoulder, tugging gently at his sweat soaked shirt "Well, you're stuck with me now. We're going to take this academy by storm, you and me!"

"For sure! I can't wait! Me and you to the end!"

Jack lies in bed that night, thinking about how far he's come in just a few short weeks. He still misses home and feels out of place sometimes, but now he has a friend by his side. Together, they're ready to face whatever challenges the academy throws their way. Which is good, as his biggest challenge is still yet to come.

5

Back Scratches
and Birdy Rumours

"Football is about sacrifice, dedication,
and the courage to keep going when things get tough."

Alan Shearer

"Come on, Jack, let's go!" Tommy shouts in a hurry.

"Five more minutes," Jack mumbles into his pillow. The morning sun peeks through the curtains, shining light on his barely open eyes.

"No, we need to go now!" Tommy barks.

"Go where?" Jack asks, propping himself up against his headboard.

"School, of course. Well, I say school. It's more just one room and a teacher. But we still learn things, so I guess it still counts," Tommy says shrugging his shoulders.

Jack blinks slowly, his half-asleep brain trying to make sense of the word school. "We have to study?" he asks.

"Of course. Our academy only accepts the best of the best, Jack. Brains on the field, brains off it," Tommy states. "Now, get a move on!"

"Okay, I'm coming, I'm coming," Jack mutters, grabbing his backpack.

As they walk down the hallway towards the education building, Wilson stops Tommy.

"Hey, Jack, you go on ahead. I need to speak with Wilson," Tommy whispers nervously.

"Um, okay. I'll save you a seat," Jack offers.

"Thanks," Tommy replies, with a slight frown.

Jack walks down the empty hallway, his footsteps echoing off the shiny white walls that remind him of a hospital. He pushes open a creaky wooden door with peeling dark brown paint at the edges. A familiar school smell hits his nose—a mix of powdery chalk dust, musty old textbooks, and the fresh pine scent of the janitor's cleaning spray. At the front of the room, a huge blackboard covers almost the entire wall, its surface dotted with tiny bits of chalk from yesterday's lessons. Three neat rows of wooden desks and chairs face the blackboard, silently waiting for students to fill them.

"Take a seat, Mr...?" the teacher asks, leaning forward.

"Jack, sir. Jack Scorer," he responds politely.

"Take a seat, Mr. Scorer. Nice to meet you," the teacher says with a smile.

As Jack sits down, Tommy enters, looking a little shaken.

"You okay?" Jack whispers, concerned.

"Yeah, I'm fine. I just hate English. I've always been bad at it," Tommy explains. "The club can't sign you if you don't pass the end-of-season exams. It's pretty important."

"Well, luckily, I'm actually pretty good at English. Just not the best at math," Jack jokes.

"No way. That's my special power," Tommy states, covering his mouth. "Maybe we can help each other."

"Yeah, that would be awesome," Jack replies jerking his head back excitedly.

The teacher's voice echoes off the walls as he asks the class to write about their favourite place.

Jack raises his hand. "Sir, you've spelt 'favourite' wrong. Isn't it F-A-V-O-R-I-T-E?"

The class bursts out laughing.

"In America, maybe. But this is England, dear lad. We add a U here," the teacher explains kindly.

Jack's cheeks flush bright red as he bows his head.

The lesson is soon over in a flash, much to Jack's relief.

Jack sighs as they leave the room. "Glad that's over. Can't believe I embarrassed myself in front of the whole class."

"It's okay. No one cares," Tommy states, trying to cheer him up. "Everyone here hates school. We're football players. They'll judge you on the field, not in the classroom. Just do the work and get the grades. It's important for the future."

"So now what?" Jack asks.

"We have a bit of time before maths class. Do you want to go to the study area to practice?" Tommy suggests. "I can help you if you like. You scratch my back, I'll scratch yours."

Jack stares at him, raising an eyebrow. "You okay?"

"Yeah, why?"

"Huh? We don't go around scratching backs in America. How's that gonna help us ace our tests?"

Tommy bursts out laughing. "No, no, it's just a saying! It means we help each other out. You know, I scratch your back, you scratch mine. Team effort!"

"Phew! I was worried for a sec. You're cool and all, but I'm not up for a back-scratching party," Jack replies with a giggle.

The two head to the study area. Pencils, notebooks, and textbooks fill the dozen or so shiny white desks, ready for their morning session. Professional footballers smile down from their frames on the study walls, showcasing the results of hard work. Today's math formulas wait on the far whiteboard in neat blue marker.

"So why did you come here, Jack?" Tommy inquires as they settle down with their books.

"I thought we came to study?" Jack remarks, holding up his book.

Tommy laughs. "I mean, why to this academy? Did your parents force you to like mine?"

"No, no, I won a competition. I found a golden ticket in a pack of trading cards. It was so lucky. It's always been my dream to be a star player," Jack admits.

"Wow, that's so cool, someone whose parents didn't force. You're rare," Tommy exclaims.

"What do you mean? Did your parents make you come here?" Jack replies.

"Well, not exactly"—Tommy pauses, staring at the players on the study hall walls. He anxiously taps his pencil on the desk—"My dad and his dad before him were both professional players. So, ever since I was little, all I've known was football. Don't think I've missed a training session since I was three."

"Wow, that must be so cool," Jack says, leaning back in his chair, impressed.

Tommy looks down, fidgeting with his hands. "Um, yeah, cool, I guess," he replies quietly. "Sometimes it can be a little much."

"Much?" Jack inquires, not understanding.

"Yeah..." Tommy starts, but before he can continue, they're suddenly interrupted by another kid, Ginger.

"Hey, did you hear the rumours about the club?" Ginger asks nervously.

"Don't listen to him, Jack. He's just a gossip," Tommy warns. "Ninety per cent of what he says is always made up."

"Yeah, but what about the other ten per cent?" Ginger jokes.

"Just spit it out! What is it, mate?" Tommy asks rolling his eyes.

Ginger looks around nervously, shuffling his feet and drumming his fingers on the desk. "I heard the academy is running out of money. If we don't finish in the top three, they might have to close it down," he whispers.

"Shut this place down? It's the oldest in the world. No chance they'd close it. Who told you this?" Tommy groans sceptically.

Ginger smirks. "A little birdy told me."

"You can talk to animals?" Jack replies raising an eyebrow.

Tommy and Ginger look at Jack before bursting into laughter. Jack looks confused but forces a smile anyway.

"Well, your little birdy must be wrong. This club is a winning machine," Tommy argues. "They haven't finished outside the top four in all their history. They won the league last season."

"Yeah, but what about this season?" Ginger states crossing his arms.

Ginger was right. Kingsdown's season hadn't started well. After three games, the team was sitting in fourteenth place, its worst start in history.

"It's not how you start. It's how you finish," Jack chimes in, trying to be positive.

"That's the spirit," Tommy says, smiling.

"Guess you're the kid from America," Ginger says, staring at Jack.

"Well done, Sherlock," Tommy teases.

"I thought his name was Ginger?" Jack says, confused.

Tommy and Ginger burst out laughing again.

"Sherlock's an English detective. I was being sarcastic," Tommy explains.

Jack stares blankly at Tommy.

"Don't worry, I'll teach you some other time," Tommy says, patting Jack's shoulder.

"Hey, aren't you both meant to be at the game?" Ginger asks pointing at the clock.

Tommy glances towards it. It's almost 3 p.m. Panic sets in.

"When's the game?" Jack urges, narrowing his eyes.

"Three p.m.! We need to go. Now!" Tommy barks.

They run through the corridor as fast as possible, stopping at the dorm to grab their kit before rushing to the changing rooms. They arrive undetected, just in time for the team news. Jack notices Tommy talking with Wilson again as the coach begins naming the starting eleven. He tries to listen when suddenly he hears his name.

"Jack, you'll be on the bench today," Coach Wilkinson announces.

Jack freezes. He can't believe it. A chance to prove himself. It may only be a friendly match, but football is football for Jack, regardless of the opponent.

No academy players make the bench this early. Some never make it at all. He finally has his chance. He's finally going to be a star.

6

The Missed Opportunity

"You miss 100% of the shots you don't take,
but every miss is a lesson that makes you stronger."

Erling Haaland

The final whistle blows, and Jack drops to his knees.

The game did not go to plan. In fact, it was a total disaster. Jack only got to play for the last five minutes of the game. With just sixty seconds left on the clock, he and Zico found a golden opportunity to score. They were through on goal, with only the keeper to beat. As the goalie rushed towards Jack, Zico screamed for the ball. He had an open goal, practically gift-wrapped and handed to him on a silver platter.

But Jack didn't listen. He didn't pass. He took the shot himself and...missed. The game ended in a dull zero-zero draw.

"Jack. A word. Now!" Coach barks, his face red like lava.

Jack trudges to Coach Wilkinson, staring at floor, his boots feeling heavier with each step.

"What on earth was that, Jack?" Coach demands, his voice stern. "We had a chance to score. All you needed to do was pass. Why did you shoot? We had an open goal!"

"Sorry," Jack mumbles, keeping his focus on the floor. "I just wanted to score."

"Football is a team game, Jack. Not a one-person show," Coach notes, letting out a small sigh. "I'm not happy, Jack. You have a lot of work to do. If you don't improve, I'm not sure there's a place for you here."

Jack's eyes start to water. He blinks hard, trying not to cry in front of his coach.

"I mean it, Jack," Coach continues. "I want to see big improvements, and fast. Otherwise, we might have to cut your time here short."

Jack cocks his head in response, not trusting himself to speak. He slumps off to the changing rooms, feeling like the world's biggest loser.

He spends the rest of the day in his room, thinking about his family and home. He remembers his friends and their fun playing in the park. He wonders if maybe he isn't good enough after all. Perhaps he should pack his bags and go home. He'd always been scared of failing and not being good enough. Now, it looks like his worst fears are finally coming true.

Jack buries his face in his pillow and lets the tears flow. He cries until he's out of tears and eventually falls into a restless sleep. Has he just blown the opportunity of a lifetime? Only time will tell.

7

Bangers, Mash
and The Bandits

"I learned my best skills playing on the streets.
That's where you discover who you really are as a footballer."

Gabriel Jesus

The following day, he wakes up to rain pounding against the window. It's like the sky is crying, too. His dreams had given him a break from his problems, but now he's back in reality, and so are all his worries.

A voice crackles over the loudspeaker. "Jack, can you come to reception?"

Confused, Jack gets dressed and heads there right away.

"Phone call for you," the receptionist says, passing the phone to Jack.

"HAPPY BIRTHDAY, JACKO!" his parents' voices explode through the phone, making Jack nearly drop it in surprise.

With all the stress, Jack completely forgot it's his twelfth birthday.

"How are things?" his mom exclaims.

"Erm...good," Jack lies, trying to sound cheerful.

"Hmm, doesn't sound good," his mom replies, her radar picking up on Jack's mood. "What's wrong, honey?"

"It's really hard, Mom," Jack admits "Way harder than I thought."

"Of course it is, honey," she replies warmly. "You're trying to become a soccer star. If it were easy, everyone would be doing it!"

"I know, but I don't even have any friends here," Jack adds sadly.

"What about your roommate?"

"Yeah, he's cool. He's my best friend here. But he's the only one."

"Well, why don't you make friends with the others?"

"I tried," Jack explains, feeling slightly silly. "But, everyone's friends with Wilson. I don't think he likes me very much."

"I'm sure he does," his dad chips in.

"He really doesn't," Jack insists.

"Whenever I try to talk to him, he either ignores me or makes fun of my accent."

"Well, who cares if he does or doesn't? You can't be friends with everyone," his dad says wisely.

"I know, I just feel a little lonely," Jack admits. "Plus, Coach told me I need to improve or else. But I don't know how or even where to start."

The phone goes silent for a moment.

"Why don't you ask Zico for some advice?" his dad suggests. "He is the team captain, after all. That's his job."

"I guess I could," Jack mutters, considering the idea.

"Anyway, we've sent you something that might cheer you up," his mom says, changing the subject.

Jack scans the reception area and spots a package with his name.

"We thought it would go well with the boots we got you," his dad adds.

Jack opens it. It's a brand-new Premier League ball!

"It's the official one, too," his dad says proudly.

"Wow, thank you so much!" Jack yells. "But...how did you afford that?"

"You let us worry about that," his dad says. "After all, what good are boots without a ball, eh?"

"Thanks, it really means a lot," Jack says.

"You mean a lot, Jack," his mom replies softly. "Now go and find Zico. You aren't giving up on your dream that easily!"

"I will," Jack promises. "Thanks, Mom and Dad. Love you. Bye!"

Jack hangs up the phone, feeling like a different person. He misses his parents and his friends, but the call has reminded him why he's here—to follow his dream. To become a football star. He has to at least try.

He decides to seek out Zico. It's lunchtime, so there's a good chance he'd be in the cafeteria. He's right. Upon entering, the smell of sausage and potato tickles his nose. He scans the room and spots Zico at the back of the hall.

"Hey, can I join?" Jack murmurs, bowing his head slightly.

"Of course! Grab a seat," Zico urges with a friendly smile.

"What's that?" Jack asks, eyeing Zico's plate like it's from another planet.

"Oh, this is the special. It's a good one today, bangers and mash," Zico declares with his mouth half full. "Can't beat it!"

Jack frowns. "What on earth is that?" He inquires.

"Oh, sorry, yeah, you're American. It's sausages, gravy, and potatoes," Zico jokes.

"Why not just call it that, then?" Jack insists.

Zico laughs. "Who knows? That's England for you."

Zico passes Jack the menu. Jack scans it, his eyes growing wider with each item.

"You eat toads and frogs here?" Jack remarks, pointing to a new item on the menu.

"Eh?" Zico exclaims, snatching the menu from him. "Oh, that's 'Toad in the Hole'!" Zico laughs. "Chill out. It's not actual toads. It's just sausages in a giant puffy pancake thing with gravy. Sounds weird, tastes awesome!"

Jack scans the menu once more. Finding another new item. "Wait, shepherd's pie? You guys eat *humans*?"

Zico bursts out laughing. "That's baked potato and minced beef! England is crazy, but not that crazy,"

"Seriously? Why can't you just name food normal stuff?" Jack groans, throwing his hands up.

"Where's the fun in that?" Zico teases.

"I think I'm just going to have the fish and chips. That is just fish and chips, right?" Jack whispers, running his hand through his hair.

Zico rocks back on his heels, his whole body shaking as he clutches his stomach. "Yeah, that one is exactly what it says on the tin."

"A tin?" Jack moans.

"Never mind." — Zico shakes his head —"So, how are things?"

"Actually, not so good," Jack mutters, his smile fading.

"How come?" Zico responds, leaning in closer.

"I'm finding all this a little bit much. Coach says I need to work on my teamwork," Jack explains. "But I have no team to work with. If I don't do something soon, then they might throw me out. Do you have any advice?"

Zico thinks for a moment, looking around the room, debating whether to tell Jack. "Well, there is one thing, but it's a bit...unusual."

Jack's beams with excitement. "I'll do anything. What is it?"

"It's also a little risky too. Are you sure?" Zico warns.

"Yes, please. I need this," Jack ducking his head briefly, with a hint of desperation.

"Well, like you, when I first arrived, I struggled too," Zico begins. "But one day, I snuck out of the academy to go for a walk to clear my head. Then I stumbled across some street kids playing football. They call themselves the Bandits."

Jack leans in closer.

"I asked to join and ended up practising with them for months," Zico continues. "They really improved my game."

"Street kids?" Jack inquires, raising an eyebrow.

Zico nods. "They play near the old supermarket. Its huge wall is perfect for their games."

"Why would you need a wall to play football?" Jack asks.

Zico grins. "You'll see." Zico's voice turns serious. "They're nice, but they can be a little wild."

Jack shrugs. "That's okay. I'll try anything at this point."

Zico scribbles on a piece of paper. "Here's the address." He grips Jack's arm. "Keep this secret. The club forbids outside football. The coach could expel you if caught. You need to be sure it's worth the risk."

Jack swallows hard. Address in hand, he feels a thrill of excitement. This may be his chance to turn things around. "Thanks."

"Be careful, mate," Zico warns. "London streets can be tough for a kid."

"I will. Thanks again, Zico," Jack whispers as he turns away.

Jack strolls slowly back to his room, contemplating his next move. Risk it and get caught? Or should he miss his only shot?

Either way, Jack's life is about to change forever.

7

Beyond Academy Walls

"Some of football's greatest talents weren't discovered in academies, but on streets and playgrounds where passion runs free and every game feels like a World Cup final."

Zlatan Ibrahimović

"Man on! Man on!" someone yells, the voice cutting through the crisp morning air like a knife.

Jack turns, immediately losing the ball.

"Switch on, Jack! I was wide open!" another frustrated voice shouts.

Jack's cheeks burn with embarrassment. He'd been so focused on the ball at his feet that he missed his teammate's run entirely.

"Sorry, I didn't have time," he pants out, trying to catch his breath.

"You need to be faster. He took the ball way too easily from you."

Jack nods, clenching his jaw. He knows he can do better. He *has* to do better.

WHAM!

The impact comes out of nowhere. One moment, Jack's on his feet; the next, he's sprawled on the ground, the taste of grass and dirt in his mouth. The world spins for a moment before coming back into focus.

"Hey, ref! That's gotta be a foul!" he yells, struggling to get up.

The coach shakes his head, his weathered face impassive. "Up you get, Jack. That's what we call a proper tackle. You gotta toughen up, kiddo!"

Jack bites back a response. He knows arguing won't help, but the unfairness of it all stings worse than his scraped knees.

"Welcome to the big leagues, Yankee," sneers Wilson, standing over Jack like a giant. "This ain't Texas anymore!"

Jack's face burns with embarrassment and anger. He pushes himself to his feet, brushing grass off his shirt. Every muscle in his body aches, a constant reminder of how hard he's been pushing himself. Coach's whistle finally pierces the air. Jack is relieved.

"Time's up! Rest up, lads. Tomorrow, we go again! Want to see better things from you, Jack."

Jack swallows hard, his chest tightening. He hasn't been himself for a while, and he knows it. The pressure is getting to him.

A couple of days have passed since Jack's conversation with Zico. He initially decided that leaving the academy isn't worth the risk. But, after this training session, he figures he might be all out of options. The memory of Zico's words still echo in his mind, tempting him with the possibility of improvement. With rumours spreading that the club may have to start cutting players because of its poor start—thirteenth place after fifteen games—he knows he has to improve. Fast.

He must find the Bandits.

Jack knows leaving the academy and playing football outside is forbidden, so he must leave undetected. He spends breakfast pushing his food around his plate, his mind working overtime to devise a fool-proof plan. Finally, it hits him. He decides the best idea would be to pretend he's going to the nearby shopping mall to buy gifts. It could be a better alibi, but it's the best he can come up with on short notice.

He's built a good relationship with the security guard, Jeff, from the States. Jeff is an ex-professional player who had his career cut short at the age of twenty-one from a bad injury. Jack often finds himself lingering at the security desk, soaking up Jeff's stories of his playing days and the tips and tricks he shares.

Jack approaches the security desk, his heart pounding so loud he's sure Jeff can hear it. He tries to keep his voice casual as he speaks. "Hey, Jeff, I'm just popping out to the mall. Is that okay?"

Jeff looks up from his crossword puzzle with raised eyebrows. "Alright, squirt. But remember, if you're gone more than three hours, I gotta tell the boss. Them's the rules," he reminds Jack, leaning back in his ever-squeaky chair.

Jack nods, forcing a smile. "I'll be as fast as lightning, don't worry," he promises, silently praying that Jeff can't see through his act.

As soon as he's out of sight of the academy, Jack pulls the crumpled piece of paper from his pocket and follows the map. His palms are sweaty, and he wipes them on his jeans as he walks. The old supermarket is close but way beyond Jack's usual academy boundaries. Since coming to England, he hasn't left the academy. When the other boys went on trips, Jack always said no, opting to spend his extra time training instead. As he ventures into unknown territory, he feels a mixture of excitement and fear.

But as he walks, he begins to enjoy being out. He's experiencing London's sights and sounds for the first time, and it's like a feast for his senses. Car horns ring, and the roads are a mix of black cabs and red double-decker buses, all driving on what Jack thinks is the wrong side of the road. He chuckles, remembering how confusing it was when he first arrived. Red phone boxes stand like forgotten guardians on street corners, reminders of a time before cell phones. The houses are squished together like sardines in a tin. Some are big, some small, all painted in different colours. English flags hang from windows, adding splashes of red and white to the urban landscape.

Jack finds himself wondering about the people who live in these homes and what their lives are like. He likes London, he decides. It's so different from home but in a good way. In what seems like no time at all, he reaches a vast, empty, abandoned supermarket. He pauses, doubt creeping in. *Is this the right place?* It looks so...desolate. For a moment, he considers turning back.

But then a rhythmic thump catches Jack's ear. Could it be? He creeps behind the building, his curiosity overcoming his caution. And there they are—three boys and a girl playing an odd game. They're taking turns kicking a ball against a wall. It's fast-paced, like football mixed with tennis. But there's no net. Or a goal.

Jack watches, fascinated. The concrete surface puzzles him. How would his studs work here? Even worse, would they even let him play?

8

SLAM: A New Game, A New Hope

"The best innovations in football come from the streets, where creativity has no limits, and every wall becomes an opportunity."

Ronaldo Nazário (R9)

As Jack stares, pondering whether or not to turn back, a player spots him. Jack freezes, feeling like a deer caught in headlights.

"Oi! Bugger off! This is our spot!" a boy yells, his voice bouncing off the walls like a ping-pong ball.

Jack's heart feels like it's about to burst. He opens his mouth to speak, but no words come out.

"You deaf, mate? Get lost!" another yells, taking a step towards Jack.

Jack stands firm, his legs shaking but his resolve strong. He's come too far to leave now. He takes a deep breath, trying to summon his courage.

A boy charges at him like an angry bull. Jack's fight or flight instinct kicks in, but words tumble out of his mouth before he can decide whether to run or stand his ground.

"Wait! I know Zico!" Jack squeaks, his voice higher than a mouse's.

The boy stops in his tracks, his eyes narrowing in suspicion. "Prove it."

Hands shaking, Jack passes him Zico's note. Time slows, and as the boy reads it, his expression becomes unreadable.

Finally, the boy looks up, a huge grin spreading across his face. "Another academy player, eh?"

Jack leans back, relief washing over him. He's passed the first test.

"Name?" the girl calls out, her tone more curious than hostile now.

"Jack," he answers, his voice steadier than his nerves.

The kids trade glances, silently judging Jack. He shifts from foot to foot, feeling under a microscope.

"Name's Kiera, mate," the girl states, cool as a cucumber. "Welcome to the Bandits' hideout."

Jack immediately senses she's the leader.

"That's Ben and Joe, twins," she continues, gesturing to two boys.

Ben grins warmly while Joe observes Jack silently, his gaze intense.

"And Ryan, our guard dog," Kiera finishes with a playful eye roll.

Brimming with enthusiasm, Ryan leaps forward. "Woof woof!" he barks, cracking up at his own silly joke. "Get it? 'Cause I'm the guard dog!"

Jack nods, intrigued by the group. They're so different from the kids at the academy. They seem free. Kinda crazy.

"Nice to meet you," he yells, cracking a smile. "What are you guys playing, by the way?" Jack asks curiously, his eyes darting to the wall where they'd been kicking the ball.

"A SLAM, newbie," Ben grins mischievously.

"SLAM?" Jack inquires, confusion written all over his face. "What's SLAM?"

"Oh, you're in for some fun, mate," Kiera jokes, exchanging knowing glances with the others. She points to a white line drawn on the concrete. "Hit the ball at the wall. Make it hard for the next player to return it before it crosses here. Ball crosses, you lose a life. Three lives each."

Jack frowns, trying to wrap his head around the rules. "How do you make it hard?"

"Up to you, mate," Kiera answers, shrugging her shoulders. "The first is spin," she states, demonstrating with an imaginary ball. "Hit with your foot's side. Makes the ball curve off the wall. Surprise direction."

"Or power." Ryan grins, miming a powerful kick. "Hit it hard. Less time to react. They might miss."

"Placement matters," Joe quietly adds, speaking for the first time. "Corners, low, or high. Harder to reach."

"'The real pro move?' Ryan chuckles, tapping his temple. "It's all about the mind game. Change your style every point. Adaptation is everything!'"

Jack gulps, suddenly realizing what he's gotten himself into. This is more challenging than he thought. But a part of him is excited by the challenge. This is exactly what he needs to improve his game.

"Ryan's our champ," Ben declares, clapping the other boy on the shoulder. "His shot's a rocket."

"Feeling brave, academy boy?" Kiera says, crossing her arms with a slight smile. "Let's see what you've got."

Jack nods, hiding his nerves behind a determined smile. "I'm in. But I've only got boots, studs don't work on concrete."

"Barefoot, it is!" Ryan laughs, already kicking off his shoes.

"Take mine," Ben offers, slipping off his shoes. "I'll watch. Four's perfect."

Kiera bounces the ball, her eyes locked on Jack. "Ready? Let's play!"

Jack takes position, praying not to embarrass himself.

Bang. Bang. Bang. Joe smashes the ball against the wall.

Jack ducks as Joe's shot whizzes overhead.

"This is hard," Jack pants out, kicking a rock on the floor.

"I know. That's the point," Kiera shouts. "The key is using your mind. Think where you're going to hit the ball before the next person has even kicked it," she advises, demonstrating with a quick flick of her foot.

"It's all about the strategy!" Ben chips in from the sidelines.

Kiera kicks off, smashing it against the wall with a resounding thud.

Ryan reacts fast, finessing it back on his left foot, creating a tricky angle for Joe.

Joe reads it, positioning himself perfectly to the right of the wall. He hits it hard, creating a near-impossible angle for Jack to follow up.

"Big chance." Ryan grins quirking an eyebrow.

The ball bounces away wide of the wall. It's Jack's turn.

"How can I hit the wall from here?" Jack moans.

"Beckham curl!" Ryan shouts. "Can you do it?"

Jack's gaze snaps to attention. "How?"

Ryan gives rapid-fires instructions: "Inside foot. Toes up. Hit low and to the side."

Jack breathes deep, focused. "Okay, well, here goes..."

He approaches, Ryan's words echoing in his mind. Now or never.

Deep breath. He runs. Foot meets ball.

BANG! It strikes the wall.

The ball curves, a perfect arc.

Everyone watches, breathless.

"Nice one, Jack!" Kiera cheers, genuine surprise in her voice.

Ryan smirks. "My amazing coaching."

A triumphant laugh escapes Jack as realization hits. "It actually worked!"

For the first time since he arrived, Jack finds himself having fun—enjoying football. Not only this, but he's also learning new skills. Time flies by, and before he knows it, he has to leave.

"Wow, guys. That was awesome. But I gotta go. Can I play with you guys again tomorrow?" Jack asks, hopeful, his earlier nervousness replaced by excitement.

"Course, mate. We pretty much live here," Kiera teases jokingly.

Jack takes a step back toward the gate, unable to stay still. "Tomorrow?" His shadow stretches long behind him in the golden afternoon light as the laughter of his new friends rings in his ears.

"For sure. See you later, mate," they all reply together.

Jack heads back, buying a small souvenir to use as his cover on his way home. His mind is buzzing with everything he's learned, every new skill he can't wait to try. Jack feels good. Better than good. He feels amazing. His first real friends. He can't wait to go back. He's almost forgotten he's breaking the rules. But he doesn't care. He feels like a real Bandit now.

8

Miracle In the Making

"Sometimes miracles aren't about scoring the perfect goal, but about eleven hearts beating together for something they believe in."

Alessandro Del Piero

For weeks, Jack keeps going back to play with the Bandits. Every day after training, he sneaks away from the academy. The Bandits are always happy to see him. They are so different from his strict coaches—loud, fun, and full of energy.

Jack loves playing their games. He can yell, mess up, and just have fun without worrying about being perfect. Jack learns new tricks that are nothing like what the academy teaches.

Day after day, Jack feels himself changing. He doesn't feel so stressed about the academy's rules anymore. Instead, he feels happy and sure of himself. The break from the academy's strict rules has recharged his batteries like nothing else. He's bursting with energy, more motivated and determined than ever before. He can't keep his excitement to himself anymore. He just has to tell someone.

One day, before training, he decides to go and find Tommy. It doesn't take long. Jack spots Wilson talking to Tommy near the lockers. He pauses, watching from a distance. Tommy looks different around Wilson—quiet and nervous, almost like he's scared. It's weird to see. Both boys come from wealthy families and started at the academy together. Jack wonders why Tommy seems so worried around Wilson.

Once Wilson leaves, Jack approaches Tommy with a smile so big that even a Cheshire cat would be jealous.

"Hey, Tommy, got some good news."

Tommy's eyes light up, leaning in closer. "Go on…."

Jack glances around, suddenly aware of their surroundings. "Er, maybe we should talk about it back in the dorm."

"Ooh, secretive," Tommy teases. "Alright, mystery boy, lead the way."

Back in their room, Jack spills everything—the Bandits, the game they play, the skills he's learned. Tommy listens, captivated.

"I'm going again," Jack announces.

Tommy's face falls. "Isn't that risky? If they catch you, they'll throw you out, you know?"

"I know, but it's amazing," Jack insists. "You should see the games they play. It's like nothing I've ever experienced before."

Tommy bites his lip, worry etched across his face. "I wish you hadn't told me that."

"Why not? We're friends, aren't we?"

A huge grin spreads across Tommy's face. "Thanks, mate."

Jack blinks, confused. "For what?"

"For saying I'm your friend. It… It means a lot."

"Don't you have loads of friends here already?"

Tommy's eyes drop to the floor. "Erm, yeah, I guess," he mumbles.

"Hey," Jack says, struck by a sudden idea. "Why don't you come with me next time?"

"No way, José," Tommy exclaims, looking like he's seen a ghost. "If my dad found out, he'd ground me until I'm a hundred! He's already breathing down my neck twenty-four-seven."

Before Jack can respond, Tommy glances at his watch and yelps.

"Blimey, we're late for training! Again! How do you always manage to do this to me?"

Laughing, they sprint to the training ground, skidding to a halt just as Coach Wilkinson blows his whistle.

"You're looking chipper, Jack," Coach observes, raising an eyebrow.

Jack grins. "Raring to go, Coach!"

As soon as training begins, a switch has been flipped. Jack uses the advice from the Bandits. Uses his mind. He's everywhere, winning challenges, keeping possession, making near-perfect passes. His teammates watch in awe, wondering what has gotten into him. When Jack's team is awarded a free kick, he steps up confidently.

"I've got this."

An older boy scoffs. "No chance, newbie. I'm the taker."

Coach Wilkinson intervenes. "Let him try."

Jack takes a deep breath, Ryan's instructions echoing in his mind. He lines up, facing the defenders and imagining the concrete wall. Front-inside foot, toes up, ankle locked. He charges forward and strikes the ball. It spins through the air, curving beautifully. Everyone holds their breath as it soars towards the goal...

BOOM!

The ball smashes against the crossbar, missing by inches.

"Impressive, Jack," the usual taker admits, jerking his head back slightly.

Coach Wilkinson claps his hands. "Very close, Jack! Well done!"

"Thanks," Jack replies, trying to hide his disappointment. "Wish it had gone in, though."

"Can't score them all," Coach states, clapping him on the back. "But that was a huge improvement. You'll be taking more of those in the future."

Jack's confidence soars. He plays the rest of the session with a newfound swagger, each touch more assured than the last. It feels like his old self is finally resurfacing.

As training ends, Coach pulls Jack aside. "Great job today, Jack! Keep playing like that, and you could go pro!"

Jack's face lights up like a Christmas tree. "Really? That would be amazing!"

"Just keep doing what you're doing," Coach encourages. "Who knows what might happen after the break? We could certainly use someone like you on the team."

As Jack returns to the dorm, he overhears some older players discussing the team's standing. They're in eleventh place—the lowest in thirty years. With rumours swirling about the club's financial troubles, it seems like they need a miracle.

Jack has a thought. Maybe, just maybe, he can be that miracle.

9

A Different Kind of Holiday

"The best gifts in football don't come wrapped in paper,
but in moments of pure joy."

Gabriel Batistuta

While most academy players head home for Christmas, Jack decides to stay put. The flights are expensive, but most importantly, Jack doesn't want to go back. He misses his family, but he's made a new family here—the Bandits.

He has continued to meet them daily since their first encounter. It's Christmas Day, and they've invited him to play a different game on their sacred ground. Only the most trusted are invited to play at "The Rec."

Jack meets them at the usual hangout, the old supermarket before they take another ten-minute walk.

"Why all the secrecy?" Jack whispers, curiosity getting the better of him.

Kiera grins mysteriously. Tapping her nose. "This is our special place."

"Can't have any weirdos knowing about our spot, can we, mate?" Ryan chips in, wiggling his eyebrows.

Ben nods seriously. "Plus, it's technically not allowed."

"Yep, but we are the Bandits, after all. We need to live up to our name," Ryan jokes.

Ten minutes later, they arrive. Jack's jaw drops.

In front of them is a huge football field that seems to go on forever, equipped with two goalposts on either side. The ground is bumpy and uneven and seems to be on a slight slope.

"You guys play here?" Jack comments, gazing around the pitch.

"Yep, our own little academy," Kiera replies smiling.

"Academy?" Jack responds, frowning.

"Goals and nets. That's all you really need," Ben insists.

Kiera smiles proudly with her hands on her hips. "Yep, it doesn't look like much, but it's our slice of heaven."

"Yeah, mate, this is where dreams come true," Ryan declares.

Joe nods quietly, a rare smile on his face.

"Plus, we can play our favourite game here," Ben says.

"What's that?" Jack asks, leaning in closer.

"WEMBLEY!" they all shout, their voices echoing across the field.

Jack scratches the back of his neck racking his brain. "Wembley? The big stadium?"

Ben chuckles. "Not the stadium. It's our game."

Kiera stands forward. "Let me explain. One person goes in goal. The goalie then kicks the ball out."

"Then it's everyone for themselves," Ryan adds, miming a tackle.

"Shut up, Ryan," Kiera barks playfully. "You then have to try and get the ball first, beat the other players, and score."

Jack's eyes grow wide with wonder as he takes it all in. "Wow, that sounds hard."

"It is." Kiera laughs. "If you score, you move to the next round. The last player left is out."

"How do I beat the other players?" Jack murmurs, rubbing the back of his neck.

Ben stands up straight. "Skill, my friend. Pure skill."

"You ready, Jack?" Ryan teases, bouncing on his toes.

A nervous laugh escapes Jack as he shifts from foot to foot, unsure how to begin.

"That's a yes!" Kiera declares. "Let's play!"

Ben boots the ball high into the air. It lands right at Jack's feet! But before Jack can move, the others charge at him like a pack of hungry wolves. The ball is gone in a flash.

"Gotta be quicker, Jack!" Kiera yells as she races away with the ball.

In seconds, Kiera has scored. She's in the next round.

Ben kicks the ball again. This time, it lands near Ryan. Ryan pushes past Joe, but Jack sees his chance and slides in with a perfectly timed tackle.

"Great tackle, Jack!" Kiera cheers from the sidelines.

"That's a foul!" Ryan yells, his face red with anger.

"No way. Keep playing!" Ben calls from the goal.

Jack doesn't need to be told twice. He takes a touch, looks up, then strikes the ball with all his might. It flies into the top corner of the goal like a rocket!

"Get in! Great goal!" Kiera shouts, giving him a high-five.

The game continues, fast and furious. Joe pulls off a fantastic move, the Maradona spin leaving Ryan in a heap on the ground before scoring a goal that slips right under Ben's arms.

"See ya, Ryan!" Kiera teases.

Ryan jumps up, brushing off his shorts. "No fair! The ground's all bumpy," he complains.

"You always say that!"

Everyone laughs, including Ryan.

Jack feels a rush of excitement. He's playing well with the Bandits!

The final round is about to start. Jack, Kiera, and Joe face off.

Ben kicks the ball high. Kiera is first to it, immediately pulling off a tricky move that leaves Jack in her dust. Joe sends her wide. She manages to get a shot out to the nearest post. Ben blocks it, pushing it to his right, leaving the ball in open play and the goal open.

Jack seizes his chance. He races to the ball and sends it into the empty net.

"Goal hanger!" Kiera laughs, half-annoyed.

"Fair game!" Ryan shouts from the sidelines.

Jack can't help but smile.

As they all flop onto the frosty green grass to catch their breath, Jack realizes just how much he's enjoying himself. This isn't just football—it's fun, pure and simple.

"Hey, guys, it's Christmas. Don't you have to go home?" Jack remarks, suddenly remembering the date.

"Not us. We're Jewish. We don't celebrate Christmas," Ben responds, speaking for Joe too.

"I don't think my parents will even notice I'm gone," Ryan states, trying to force a smile.

"Christmas isn't that fun for me anymore," Kiera replies softly. Turning away slightly. "Ever since my dad passed away a few years ago, it hasn't been the same. More time away from the house, the better for me."

Jack falls silent, not knowing what to say.

"It's okay, Jack," Kiera continues, her voice stronger. "He was sick for a while. It wasn't sudden. But it wasn't nice either. My mum didn't take it well, so I had to look after my little brother for a while, but she's better now. Well, most of the time," she adds, a hint of doubt in her voice. "What about you, Jack?" Kiera asks, changing the subject. "Why aren't you heading back home?"

"Erm, my family couldn't afford it," Jack explains. "Plus, I've just started liking it here. I need all the practice I can get."

Jack glances at his watch and jumps up. "I better be going. Jeff only lets me out for three hours."

"Ok catch you later mate!" the bandits shout as Jack gets up to leave.

Jack can't stop grinning as he says his goodbyes and jogs away.

Little does he know, this Christmas Day game is just the beginning of an adventure that would test his skills, loyalty, and dreams in ways he never imagined possible.

10

From Bench to Brilliance

"The harder you work, the luckier you get."

Gary Lineker

The rest of the Christmas holidays fly by in a blur of football, laughter, and new friendships. Jack continues to meet the Bandits, each session leaving him stronger, faster, and more skilled than before. It isn't just his football skills that are improving; Jack finds himself growing more confident, more assertive. Jack is no longer afraid to call for the ball. In fact, he's started to outright demand it.

His time at the Rec also makes him a better team player. Coach Wilkinson notices this transformation too. He's under pressure to turn the team's fortunes around. The team has come back from the break, but victory still eludes them. They've lost their first two games since returning, making it ten losses in a row. The situation is dire—the team needs a hero. They need Jack.

All that extra practice over the break has turned Jack into a football wizard. In training, he's everywhere at once—snatching up loose balls like a vacuum cleaner, passing with laser-like precision, and finding the back of the net with almost every shot. It's as if he's been touched by football magic.

Coach Wilkinson watches Jack's progress with growing excitement. Finally, he makes a decision that will change everything.

"Hey, Jack, can I have a word?" Coach whispers after a particularly gruelling training session.

"Yeah, sure," Jack replies, shrugging his shoulders.

Coach's face breaks into a wide grin. "Just want to say well done on your improvement. I don't know what you're doing, but it's working, so keep it up."

"Thanks, Coach," Jack says, a warmth of pride spreading through his chest.

"Oh, one more thing, Jack," Coach adds. "Make sure you rest well tonight. Tomorrow, you'll be starting your first game."

Jack's jaw drops. He can't believe his ears. Starting for the first team? That's unheard of for a first-year academy player! As the news sinks in, Jack feels a volcano of excitement and nerves bubbling up inside him. This is it. His dream is coming true.

The next day soon arrives and it's game time.

Jack steps onto the pitch, to a massive round of applause. He takes in the soft, bouncy grass beneath him, the smell of hot dogs wafting through the air, and a gentle breeze brushing his face. He waves to what feels like a million people in the crowd, trying to conceal his shaky hands. As he moves to the centre circle, he gives Zico a reassuring nod, then looks up and gestures broadly to the audience. Jack clenches his fists, preparing to show the whole stadium what he's made of as the whistle blows.

The first half unfolds well. Tommy and Zico dominate the midfield, leaving the opposition with no room to breathe. Jack receives the ball on the edge of the box and strikes it first time—but it goes just inches wide. Jack is relentless; wherever the ball goes, he chases after it. The crowd roars, clapping in appreciation for his evident work rate. It's infectious, and soon the entire team chases every loose ball. They eventually earn a corner kick, taken by Zico and swung in with pace. A misplaced header from the opposition allows the ball to drop directly at Jack's feet on the penalty spot. He takes one touch, then—boom! Goal! His first for Kingsdown flies straight into the top left corner, leaving the goalie frozen in place. Jack feels ecstatic, shaking his fists at the roaring crowd.

Deep into the second half, Jack builds his match fitness but starts to tire, dropping his shoulders and panting as if he's in an all-you-can-eat air buffet. The coach signals that it's time for him to come off. Jack puts his hands on his hips and lowers his head. However, as he walks off the pitch, the crowd lifts his spirits with a huge round of applause. "Scorer, scorer!" rings out around the stadium. The coach gives Jack a firm nod of approval and a strong pat on the back. Jack knows he has passed his first audition.

With Jack's debut ending in a 1-0 victory, the team's losing streak is finally broken. The following weeks get even better, like a roller coaster that only goes up. Jack continues to shine brighter than a diamond. It's as if he has golden boots, as he scores in each of the next six games! His goals act like rocket fuel, propelling the team to eighth place in the league after twenty-five games. It's almost magical—the more he practices with the Bandits, the better he plays for Kingsdown.

Soon, Jack isn't just a super sub anymore. He's a regular starter, the first name on the team sheet. The whole team plays better with Jack in it. His energy is infectious, his passion inspiring. It's as if his presence alone has made everyone raise their game.

Well, almost everyone. One player doesn't seem to be enjoying Jack's meteoric rise—Wilson.

Wilson has been a regular starter all season and the season before. He plays in the same position as Jack, and with Jack on such a hot streak, Wilson finds himself warming the bench more often than not. Wilson has never liked Jack much to begin with, but now his dislike is turning into something uglier. Every time Jack scores, Wilson's scowl deepens. Every time Coach praises Jack, Wilson's fists clench a little tighter.

But Jack doesn't let it bother him. He's focused on football and his goal of becoming a star player. He's worked too hard, come too far to let anything or anyone distract him now.

11

The Tunnel Ambush

"Obstacles don't have to stop you.
If you run into a wall, don't turn around and give up."

Didier Drogba

It's late January, and the second half of the football season is in full swing. The club is still in eighth place, but they're climbing up the table, primarily thanks to Jack's superb form. Jack feels settled. His daily routine is as regular as clockwork. He wakes up, trains with the academy, hits the books with Tommy, munches some lunch, and sneaks out for three hours of playtime with his street football buddies.

After that, it's back for dinner and off to Dreamland. He calls his parents sometimes, too, but because he wants to, not because he's homesick. With the Bandits, Tommy, and chatting with Jeff, the friendly security guard, Jack feels like he's found a whole new family right here in London. Life's pretty sweet for Jack.

One day, Jack heads out as usual. He's off to the Rec to play Wembley doubles with the Bandits. It's like regular Wembley, but they play in pairs. This game's been a real game-changer for Jack's teamwork skills—exactly what he needs to be a star player. The game goes well. Jack paired up with Ben and they end up beating Kiera and Ryan. But it's Jacks return to the academy where things start to go a little pear-shaped.

As Jack makes his way back to the academy, he approaches a long tunnel. It's like a train tunnel but shorter, with a ceiling high enough to play basketball. He strolls through, whistling a happy tune, without a care in the world when four older boys pop out of nowhere, blocking his path like a wall of grumpy giants.

"You Jack?" growls one boy wearing a black mask that makes him look like a wannabe superhero villain.

"Uh, that's me," Jack squeaks, his voice as high as a mouse. "What's up, guys?"

"Hand over the fancy boots, Yankee Doodle," the leader demands.

"I can't," Jack protests, his voice shaking like jelly. "My parents got them for me. They're super special. I need 'em for soccer... I mean, football. I play at the acad—"

"*Shut up!*" the leader roars. "We don't care. We're not asking, kid. We're telling you!"

"Easy way or hard way," another boy adds, cracking his knuckles like he's getting ready for a fight.

Jack's scared stiff. He shakes. These kids are older, bigger, and meaner.

He thinks about making a run for it, but they're blocking both ends of the tunnel. He can't risk getting hurt. He's got no choice.

"Here you go," Jack whispers, as he hands over his beloved red Ronaldo boots.

The leader grins. "See? Not so hard. Now beat it. Don't come around here again. Go!" the leader yells, his voice echoing through the tunnel like angry thunder.

Jack takes off like a rocket, his feet slapping against the cold ground. His heart's pounding faster than a drum at a rock concert. He zooms past Jeff, the guard, through the building and locks himself in his room. Jack dives onto his bed and buries his face in his pillow, crying his eyes out.

Before long, the door opens, and Tommy enters.

"What's wrong, Jack?" Tommy asks creeping closer.

"Go away. I don't want to talk," Jack mumbles into his pillow.

"Erm, okay, mate."

Tommy leaves, immediately closing the door behind him.

Jack is left scared and alone, wondering if he has just blown the biggest opportunity of a lifetime.

12

A Captains Wisdom

"Leadership isn't about wearing the armband,
it's about lifting others up."

Roberto Firmino

Days pass, and Jack skips training. He knows he has to stay away; if Coach discovers why he has no boots to play with, due to his sneaking out, he gets expelled from the academy immediately. The number one rule is no outside football. To buy some time, Jack puts on his best sick act, complete with fake coughs and sniffles.

But after a week of staying room bound, everyone begins to worry.

Everyone except Tommy that is. He's no fool. He knows Jack's illness is about as real as a three-dollar bill. He knows something bad went down. So he calls in the big guns and asks Zico for help.

Knock-knock.

"Jack? You in there?" Zico whispers.

"Go away. I'm sick." He snaps, faking a cough that sounds about as convincing as a dog trying to meow.

"Jack, you don't have to pretend. I know," Zico insists.

The door creaks open a smidge. Jack peeks out, looking like a scared rabbit.

"You know what?" Jack murmurs.

"Your boots," Zico states, pointing at Jack's feet.

Jack panics and tries to slam the door shut, but Zico jams his foot in to stop him.

"It's okay. I won't tell. I want to help," Zico insists.

Jack lets him in, looking like he's about to cry again. "How did you know about the bullies who took my boots?"

"Bullies? I didn't know about that. But I knew something was up with your boots because I talked to Jeff," Zico explains. "He saw you running in barefoot. People don't usually do that. Well, not the normal ones anyway," he jokes, trying to lighten the mood.

Jack cracks a smile for the first time since it happened. "Some older kids cornered me on my way back," Jack admits. "They knew my name and said to give them my boots or else. So I did. Now I'm stuck here. If Coach finds out I left, I'll be a goner. Plus, I told the Bandits I'd meet them. Now I haven't seen them for a week. They've probably forgotten about me," Jack states, looking sadder than a puppy left out in the rain. "I don't know what to do. Maybe I should just quit. Maybe it's a sign," Jack cries, wiping away a tear.

Zico thinks for a bit. "That's rough, Jack. But you can't stay cooped up in here. If you do, they'll think you're really sick. They might send you home."

Jack puts his head in his hands.

"I've got an idea," Zico urges, his eyes lighting up like a Christmas tree. "My mom's under the weather, so Coach gave me two weeks off to visit her in back home. Your feet are about the same size as mine. Why don't you borrow my boots? It's only for two weeks. But it gives you more time."

"But then what?" Jack remarks, tightening his lips.

"Well, who knows? In the worst case, you get to play two more weeks of football. Best case? Some miracle happens, and you'll play here forever. It's better than nothing, right?"

Jack nods, a tiny spark of hope flickering in his eyes. "It's not just that, though. I can't stop thinking about it. My mind feels like it's going to explode. I dream about it, then as soon as I wake up, I think about it. I'm angry, sad, and worried all at once. I feel so stressed out."

Zico pats him on the back, his hand gentle as a feather. "Hey, it's okay to feel that way, Jack. I've been there too."

"You have?" Jack replies, looking up with eyes as big as footballs.

"Yeah, I mean, I didn't have my boots stolen. But I've been through tough times where I couldn't stop thinking about bad things."

"Like what?" Jack murmurs.

Zico pauses, taking a deep breath like he's about to dive into a pool. "Well, I've never told anyone this story. But years ago, before the academy, I lived in Brazil. My family was poor and often had to work, so my grandpa looked after me most of the time. Every weekend, we'd watch Flamengo play."

"Flamengo?" Jack chuckles. "Sounds like a bird!"

Zico grins. "It does. But it's one of the biggest clubs in Brazil. I loved going to the stadium. It was the highlight of my week. Every time at the stadium, I felt...home. Part of something bigger."

Zico leans closer to Jack, his voice dropping to a whisper. "Inside, everyone became family. Rich, poor, rivals, it didn't matter. The whistle blew, and bam! All brothers. All together on one side."

Jack listens, fascinated as if Zico's telling the most amazing bedtime story ever.

Zico narrows his eyes. "Songs, referee rants, shouting at the players—but love for the club united them all."

His voice gets quieter. "For ninety minutes, I belonged. My troubles were gone. I was safe. I was home. I would always joke with Grandad that one day I would be on the pitch, not in the stands. But..."

Zico's smile fades like a setting sun. "But then Grandad died. So, the games stopped. I missed it. I missed him. I couldn't stop thinking about him. So my mom told me to write down everything I felt. I did, and I felt better. I've been doing it ever since."

"Write them down?" Jack inquires.

"Yeah, like in a journal or notebook," Zico explains. "All my thoughts and feelings for the day. What I did well, what I didn't. Where I could do better. What I'm thankful for. I just wrote it all down. When I did, the bad thoughts stopped."

"Really? That worked?" Jack remarks.

"Yep, sure does. Think of your brain like a full computer. The journal is like a printer. Start printing things out, and your brain suddenly has more space. Space for good stuff. I still do it now, even when I'm not sad. It's really helped my football. With no bad thoughts, I can focus just on the game. That's how I became captain. You need a clear head for that."

"Wow, thanks, Zico," Jack responds, sitting up straighter.

"No problem. You rest up. I'll leave my boots by your door before I leave tomorrow. Take good care of them. Remember, training only, okay? We can't both get thrown out," Zico jokes.

"Don't worry, I won't," Jack says, smiling like he's just won the World Cup.

"See you later, Jack," Zico shouts as he leaves, closing the door softly behind him.

Jack flops back on his bed, staring at the ceiling as if it holds all the answers in the universe. He still doesn't know exactly what he's going to do, but he feels better, as if a storm cloud has just cleared from his brain.

Hearing Zico's story and advice has lit a fire in Jack's belly. He's worked too hard to give up because of some mean bullies. Plus, he's got Zico's secret weapon to try out—the journal.

13

The Mystery Package

"In football, like in life, it's not about the gifts you receive,
but the meaning behind them. A pair of boots can carry
more than just your feet - they can carry friendship, hope,
and forgiveness."

Romelu Lukaku

Jack jogs onto the training field. It's his first day back, and boy, does it show. His passes are short, and his shots are poor at best. The team could also be doing better. Before Jack's little "incident," Kingsdown was on fire, winning game after game. But while Jack was away, they drew one match and lost another.

Zico's boots are doing the job, but there's a problem: Zico would be back in just a couple of days. Jack is running out of time. But just when he thinks all hope is lost, something very unexpected happens.

The day before Zico is due back, Jack gets a message from the security office. There's a package waiting for him.

"Huh?" Jack scratches his head. He hasn't ordered anything, and his parents always warn him before sending stuff. Jack heads to the gate, where he finds Jeff, the friendly security guard, grinning like a Cheshire cat.

"Well, well, well! Look who it is!" Jeff chuckles. "Long time no see, Jack!"

"Hey, Jeff." Jack smiles sheepishly., staring at the floor. "Yeah, I've had some...stuff going on."

Jeff bobs his head, rolling his eyes. "I see, I see. Well, this arrived for you today."

He hands Jack a big cardboard box.

"What is it?" Jack asks, eyeing the package suspiciously.

Jeff laughs. "How should I know? It's your package!!"

Jack tears into the box like it's Christmas morning. When he sees what's inside, his jaw drops so far it nearly hits the floor.

"No way..." he whispers.

Inside the box is a brand-spanking new pair of football boots. But not just any boots—they're exactly like his old ones!

"I don't get it," Jack exclaims, his brain doing somersaults. "How did you know?"

Jeff holds up his hands. "Whoa there, kiddo! These aren't from me. I'm just the delivery guy." He winks at Jack. "Let's just say you've got some pretty awesome friends around here."

Jack peers into the box again and spots a note. It reads: "No star should ever be without their boots. Especially a star of the Bandits."

Jack gasps. The Bandits? How did they even know about his boot drama?

Jeff hisses before he can ponder this mystery further. "Psst! Coach alert! Hide the goods!"

Jack shoves the box behind his back just as Coach rounds the corner.

"There you are, Jack!" Coach states. "I've been looking all over for you!"

A cold feeling washes over Jack. Has his secret been found out? Is Coach going to send him home? Is this the end of his Kingsdown career?

But Coach's following words surprise him.

"I know you've been under the weather lately, but we have a huge game tomorrow. It's do-or-die time, and the team's been struggling without you. I need you back in the starting line-up."

Jack tilts his head in agreement, looking casual while hiding a giant box behind his back.

"So, what do you say, hotshot?" Coach asks with a grin. "Ready to be our secret weapon and save the day?"

A grin spreads across Jack's face. "One hundred percent, Coach!"

"That's what I like to hear!" Coach claps him on the shoulder. "See you bright and early tomorrow, Jack!"

As Coach walks away, Jack lets out a massive sigh of relief. "Phew! That was way too close!"

"You're telling me!" Jeff agrees. "Listen, Jack, I can't let you leave the academy again, okay? It's just too risky. You got lucky this time, and so did I!"

Jack's face falls. "But...I need to thank them."

Jeff shakes his head. "I know, buddy, but remember why you're here. You can't become a star if they ship you back to America, right?"

"I guess not," Jack mumbles.

"Don't worry," Jeff says with a wink. "I'll make sure your friends know you got the package. Now hurry! You've got a big game to prepare for!"

Jack gives Jeff a quick hug. "Thanks, Jeff. You're the best!"

"Alright, alright." Jeff laughs, playfully shooing Jack away. "Enough of that mushy stuff. Go on, get out of here!"

Jack sprints back to his room, his head spinning. An hour ago, he thought he was toast. Now he's got new boots and a chance to play in tomorrow's big game! As he paces around his room, buzzing with excitement, one question keeps popping into his head: How did the Bandits know about the boots? At first, he thinks maybe Zico had something to do with it. But Zico's in Brazil! And Jeff said it wasn't him...so who could it be?

Jack scratches his head, confused. But he pushes the worry away for now. He's got something way more exciting to think about—his first big game since the whole boot disaster! As he brushes his teeth and puts on his pajamas, Jack can't believe how close he came to losing everything he cared about. His mind races with thoughts of football. He pictures himself scoring amazing goals and becoming a superstar.

NUMBER 9: THE BEGINNING | Jack Scorer

Jack smiles at his reflection in the mirror. Tomorrow's game is his chance to show everyone what he's truly capable of!

14

From Triumph to Tragedy

"The highest highs and lowest
lows often come hand in hand."

Romário

Jack bursts onto the field like a superhero, his return sparking a wave of excitement. It's like he was never away. His passes are crisp. Everyone executes with pinpoint accuracy. He chases every second ball like a dog with a bone. Spotting opposition runs and cutting them out. Darting left, right and centre with defence-splitting runs. Scoring twice before it's even half-time!

In the second half, the opposition tries to scare Jack, charging at him like a herd of angry bulls. But Jack stays as cool as a cucumber, simply calming his mind. Looking up and playing the perfect pass. Before he knows it, the game is over. Jack not only scored two goals that game but also grabbed an assist, his first of the season, with the team winning three-zero.

Before Jack's comeback, the team felt pretty down in the dumps. But Jack's comeback rejuvenated the team. They saw his determination and matched it. The whole team is on fire! Jack follows Zico's advice, journaling every day and taking deep breaths before a game. It's was a game-changer. Jack is on a hot streak with a head as clear as the blue sky above, scoring an incredible ten goals in just five games! That includes his first-ever hat-trick—three goals in one game.

The team's five-game winning streak and Jack's red-hot form catapult them up to seventh place. With only ten games left, they're just seven points behind the top spot. Suddenly, winning the whole league doesn't seem like such a crazy idea after all!

After a nail-biting two-one win against the fourth-place team, Jack is called to the office. His parents are on the phone.

"Hey, Mom!" Jack chirps. "Guess what? I scored twice today! We won two-one!"

"That's fantastic, honey!" his mom replies. "We're so proud of you."

"Yeah, I've been using those cool mind tricks Zico taught me. They're really helping my game!"

"That's wonderful, Jack," his dad chimes in. "We're thrilled everything's going so well."

Jack bounces on his toes. "It really is! So...what's up? You guys normally only call on Sundays. You know I play on Saturdays now."

There's a pause on the other end of the line. When his parents speak again, their voices sound different. Sad, almost.

"Are you okay?" Jack whispers softly. "You sound upset."

His mom takes a deep breath. "We've got some news, Jack. It's about Jake."

Jack gets excited. Jake, his faithful dog and best buddy since forever. "Oh, cool! Put him on! I love hearing his goofy bark!"

Another pause. "We have some bad news, sweetie," his mom says softly.

Jack's smile fades. His bouncing stops. "What? Why? What happened?"

His dad speaks up. "We were at the park yesterday, and Jake...well, you know how he loves chasing birds."

Jack nods, even though his parents can't see him. "Yeah, he's crazy about birds!"

"Well," his dad continues, "he saw one and ran off after it. But...he ran onto the road, and a car... Well, a car hit him."

Jack gasps, worry flooding his face. "Is he hurt? Did you take him to the vet?"

His mom's voice is barely a whisper. "I'm so sorry, honey. It happened so fast. Jake... He didn't make it."

The world seems to stop spinning. Jack can't breathe. Can't think.

"No," he mutters. "No, that can't be true."

"We're so sorry, Jack," his dad says. "We know how much Jake meant to you."

Tears start rolling down Jack's cheeks. "If I was there, I could've stopped him! He always listened to me!"

"Oh, sweetie," his mom states gently. "It wasn't your fault. These things... They happen sometimes."

Jack can barely speak through his sobs. "I... I need to go."

"We love you, Jack," his parents say. "Take care of yourself, okay?"

Jack hangs up the phone and races back to his room. He throws himself on his bed, burying his face in his pillow. All the memories come flooding back: Jake waiting by the door every day when Jack came home from school, Jake protecting him from bullies in the park, and Jake teaching him to play "doggy football." The worst part is the guilt. Jack wasn't there when Jake needed him, so he didn't get to say goodbye. He's never felt so alone.

Just then, Tommy walks in.

"Hey, Jack, I just learned a really cool football move. Do you want to see it?"

Jack doesn't respond.

"Jack?"

"I don't care," Jack mumbles into his pillow.

The room goes quiet.

"Hey," Tommy says softly. "What's wrong? You can talk to me, you know. We're best friends."

He's right. Jack and Tommy have gotten super close. They help each other with homework, training, and just about anything. They always have each other's backs.

Jack sits up slowly, his eyes red and puffy. "It's Jake. My dog. He's... He's gone."

"Gone?" Tommy responds, confused. "You mean, like, ran away?"

Jack shakes his head. "No, he's... He died. And it's all my fault!"

"Whoa, hold on," Tommy murmurs, sitting next to Jack. "What happened?"

Between sobs, Jack tells Tommy the whole story.

When he finishes, Tommy puts a hand on his shoulder. "I'm so sorry, mate. That's awful."

Jack wipes his eyes. "He was my oldest friend. My first best friend. And now he's gone because of my stupid dream of being a football star!"

Tommy is quiet for a moment. "Can I tell you a secret? I've never told anyone this before."

Jack looks up, curious despite his sadness. "Okay."

Tommy takes a deep breath. "Well, I had a pet once. His name was Harold. He was a bird."

"Your parents let you have a pet?" Jack replies, raising an eyebrow.

Tommy shakes his head. "No way. They said it would distract me from football. But I wanted one so bad. I wished for one every single day."

"Then what happened?"

"One day, this bird just showed up at my window. I opened it, and he flew right in and sat on my bed! At first, I was scared. But then I started talking to him. My parents were always too busy to talk, but Harold? He always had time for me."

Jack listens intently, leaning in closer.

"Every day for five years, Harold would come to my window at exactly 7 a.m. It was like magic!"

"But then what?" Jack whispers.

Tommy's face falls. "One day, my friend invited me for a sleepover. My first ever! It was awesome...until I woke up and realized I hadn't opened the window for Harold. I ran home as fast as possible, but it was too far. By the time I got there, it was way past seven."

"What happened to Harold?" Jack asks.

Tommy's voice grows quiet. His face turns white. "He never came back. I opened that window every single day after, but...nothing. I blamed myself. I thought maybe Harold thought I didn't like him anymore because I didn't open the window. If I hadn't gone to that stupid sleepover, maybe he'd still be around."

The room goes quiet again.

"I told my grandma about it," Tommy says after a while. "She's the only one in my family who's not always super busy. And you know what she told me?"

Jack shakes his head.

"She said birds are free, just like us. They go wherever they want. Maybe Harold found some cool bird friends, or maybe he found an awesome new place to hang out. Or something not so good happened. Something nobody could stop." Tommy looks at Jack. "What I'm trying to say is...we can't control everything, Jack. It's like...your dog loved chasing birds, right? That's what made him happy. And you love football. That's your thing. We can't always be there to watch everything we care about. It's just...not possible, you know?"

Jack dips his chin, the tears starting to slow. "But I can't stop thinking about him," he states softly.

"That's a good thing," Tommy replies. "It means he'll never really leave you. He's...in a different place now. Chasing birds in doggy heaven or something."

Jack can't help but smile a little at that image despite everything.

Tommy stands up. "I'll give you some space. But remember what my grandma always says: Don't be sad it's over. Be happy it happened."

As Tommy reaches the door, Jack calls out, "Tommy!"

Tommy turns around.

"Thanks," Jack mumbles.

Tommy smiles and nods before leaving the room.

As the door closes, Jack thinks about Tommy's words. They make him feel a little better. Even though he's sad about losing Jake, he's glad he has a friend like Tommy.

15

The Comeback Kings

"It's not about falling down; it's
about getting back up every time."

Samuel Eto'o

J ack sits on his bed, staring at the wall. It's been two weeks since he heard about Jake, and his heart still feels like a part of it has been stolen. He's missed the last couple of games and does not feel up to playing. But without Jack, the team is struggling. They've lost their last two matches, three-zero and five-zero. Now, winning the league seems as likely as finding a unicorn in the locker room.

Jack's walking down the hallway when he hears voices from the manager's office. The door's open a tiny crack. Jack knows he shouldn't, but he can't help himself. He leans in to listen.

"It's true," the owner declares, his voice shaky. "If we don't finish third, we'll have to close the academy. We can't afford to keep it running."

The owner sounds sad, just like Jack felt when he lost Jake. He realizes the club is like the owner's pet—he's had it for over fifty years! Suddenly, Jack feels a surge of energy. His sadness transforms into determination. This kind old man gave Jack the chance of a lifetime, and now it's Jack's turn to help him. Without thinking, Jack races back to his room. He grabs his boots and sprints to the training field.

The grass is empty—everyone else finished practice hours ago. But Jack doesn't care. He starts running drills, dribbling between cones, and taking shots at the empty goal.

"Mind if I join?" a voice calls out. It's Tommy.

"What are you doing here?" Jack inquires, tilting his head.

Tommy puts his hands on his hips and grins. "I could ask you the same thing! Come on, let's practice together."

For the next week, Jack and Tommy train like never before. They work on passing, shooting, and fancy footwork. Soon, they're so in sync that they can read each other's minds on the field!

Their hard work pays off. In their next game, the coach puts them both in the starting line-up for the first time. It's a tough match. The other team is right behind them in the rankings. If Jack and Tommy's team loses, they can kiss their dreams of finishing third goodbye.

But Jack and Tommy are determined not to let that happen, playing their heart out and winning the game three-one! Jack scores two goals, and Tommy assists all three. They're unstoppable!

The team goes on a winning streak, winning the next three games two-zero, four-one, and one-zero. Jack and Tommy are on fire, scoring and assisting in every match. Now they're in fifth place, just three points away from that crucial third spot. Only four games are left, but suddenly, everyone believes they can do it! The whole team starts joining Jack and Tommy for extra practice. They feel like the Avengers when they play together. Well, almost everyone...

16

The Betrayal

"In football, like in life, loyalty and trust are everything."

Wayne Rooney

When Jack first arrived, his teammates took some time to warm up to him, as was expected. But eventually, they accepted him as a vital part of the team. However, one teammate, Wilson, just wouldn't take to Jack. Whether it was pushing in front of him at lunch, bumping his table during study time, delivering harsh tackles on the pitch, or simply being outright rude, Wilson remained indifferent to Jack. If anything, his attitude grew colder.

As Jack's performance improved, Wilson found himself spending more time on the bench than on the field, which only fueled his resentment towards Jack. Despite Jack's attempts to be friendly, their relationship continued to deteriorate. Unfortunately for Jack, things were about to take an unexpected turn.

The sun beats down on the training pitch as Tommy and Jack practice passing drills.

They're lost in their football world when a shout breaks their concentration.

"Tommy! Over here, now!" Wilson's voice booms from the tunnel.

Tommy winces. "Sorry, Jack. I'll be right back."

"You don't have to go," Jack says, frowning. "He's not your boss."

"I know, but...it's complicated," Tommy mumbles, jogging towards Wilson.

Jack narrows gaze and watches from a distance, puzzled. Ever since he arrived at the academy, Wilson seems to have some strange power over Tommy. Curiosity gets the better of Jack. He inches closer, trying to hear what's going on. He can't distinguish the words, but it looks like an argument.

Suddenly, Wilson shoves Tommy hard. Tommy stumbles and falls. Without thinking, Jack sprints over.

"Hey! Back off!" he yells, surprising even himself with his bravery.

Wilson sneers. "Oh, look, it's the American hero. What are you gonna do, throw a hamburger at me?"

"It's okay, Jack," Tommy says, scrambling to his feet. "Let's just go."

"No way," Jack says firmly. "This has to stop."

"Aww, how cute," Wilson mocks. "Defending your little buddy."

"Shut up, Wilson," Jack snaps. "You're just mad because we're playing, and you're stuck warming the bench."

Wilson's face turns as red as a tomato. "Watch it, new kid," he growls.

"Or what?" Jack shoots back. "Face it, Wilson. Nobody likes you here."

"Tommy does," Wilson says with a smirk. "We were best buds before you showed up."

Jack rolls his eyes. "Yeah, right."

"It's true," Wilson insists. "In fact, Tommy's been helping me this whole time."

"What are you talking about?" Jack's forehead wrinkles as he tries to make sense of it.

Wilson's grin grows wider. "Remember your precious boots that were stolen? I arranged that. And guess who was my secret spy, telling me all about your little adventures outside the academy? Your best friend, Tommy, that's who!"

"You're such a liar!" Jack yells out.

"Really? Why don't you ask him then?" Wilson replies standing with his hands on his hips lifting his chin slightly towards Tommy.

He turns to Tommy, who's staring at the ground. "Tommy? Is this true?"

Tommy looks up, his eyes watery. "Jack, I can explain—"

The truth hits Jack like a badly timed tackle, stealing both his breath and his balance. All those practice sessions, late-night talks, shared dreams spin through his mind like a tainted highlight reel. His throat closes as if trying to trap the friendship inside, refusing to let it escape into the space between them. Even the familiar smell of grass and leather from the training ground seems to mock him now. "You've been spying on me?" Jack whispers, his voice cracking. "I thought we were friends!"

"We *are* friends!" Tommy insists. "I was scared. I didn't know what to do—"

"Save it," Jack shouts, backing away. "I can't believe this."

Anger bubbles up inside him. Without thinking, he lunges at Wilson. They tumble to the ground, a tangle of fists and shouts.

"Stop it!" Tommy yells, trying to pull them apart.

Wilson manages to pin Jack down.

"Not so tough now, are you?" he taunts.

Just as Wilson raises his fist, Tommy grabs his arm. "That's enough!"

Wilson whirls around, shocked. "What do you think you're doing?"

"The right thing," Tommy states, his voice shaky but determined. "For once."

Wilson laughs. "Oh, please. You don't have the guts."

"Yes, I do," Tommy warns. He turns to Jack. "I'm so sorry, Jack. I'll explain everything, I promise."

But Jack's had enough. He pushes himself up, brushing grass off his shorts.

"Don't bother," he says coldly. "I trusted you, Tommy. We were supposed to be a team."

"We are! We still can be!" Tommy pleads.

Jack shakes his head. "No. We can't. I don't want to see either of you ever again."

With that, he turns and stalks away, ignoring Tommy's calls. As he heads down the tunnel, Jack feels his world crumble. Everything had been going so well, and now...

He wonders if anything will ever be the same again.

17

The Lonely Star

"The greatest lesson football taught me wasn't how to score goals, but how to turn loneliness into leadership. Every star player goes through moments of feeling alone - it's what you learn from those moments that matters."

Fernando Torres

Two weeks have flown by since Jack found out about Tommy. He initially tried to leave the academy but was told that if he left before his contract ended, he would have to pay for the flight home. Jack's family doesn't have much money, so after a long talk with his parents and the coach, Jack decides to stay for the last month. He's moved to a new dorm and now has a private room. It's as quiet as an empty stadium.

But this only makes Jack feel lonelier. Tommy and Jack had been inseparable. Tommy was the only person Jack talked to. He would speak to Zico, too. But Zico is captain. He has responsibilities and is often busy. Jack finds himself alone more and more.

Not only this, but the unstoppable on-field partnership between Jack and Tommy has come to a screeching halt. Tommy hasn't made an assist, and for the first time since he broke into the first team, Jack hasn't scored. There have been chances, but Jack refused to pass to Tommy. Every time Tommy tries to pass to Jack, Jack would move out of the way, giving the ball to the other team. This often results in a goal for the opposition, leaving their team feeling deflated.

Because of this, the team has drawn and lost their past two games. Now, they're in fifth place, two points behind fourth and three points behind the vital third spot. The academy needs to stay open and have a team next year.

With just two games left and the academy's future hanging by a thread, time is running out to save the club.

One day, as Jack is walking down the hallway, his feet dragging, he bumps into Jeff, the friendly security guard.

"Hey, Jack, what's up, mate? It has been a while since I've seen you. You okay? You look sad," Jeff asks, concerned.

"Yeah, I'm okay," Jack responds, trying to end the conversation quickly.

"Really? You don't look okay. Come with me. I'm about to grab some lunch from the cafeteria."

Jack hesitates to answer.

"Hey, I'm not taking no for an answer," Jeff jokes, his smile warm.

"Umm, okay," Jack agrees, shrugging his shoulders.

They walk down the hallway and enter the cafeteria. A mix of vegetable and gravy smells swirl through the air.

"Smells nice. Looks like we've got a roast today," Jeff declares whilst soaking his Yorkshire pudding in a dollop of gravy before cramming it into his gaping mouth.

"A roast?" Jack inquires, confused.

"Oh, yes. Can't beat a roast on a Sunday. It's as British as the Queen drinking tea." Jeff mumbles with a mouth half full.

Jack frowns and raises his eyebrows while waving his hands dismissively at the strange-looking contents of Jeff's overflowing plate.

"Hey its not that bad! Potato, carrots, onions, broccoli, Yorkshire puddings, beef, and a dollop of gravy," Jeff decares, pointing at each item. "Can't beat it."

They both grab a tray and begin to eat.

"So, how have you been, Jack? It's been a while," Jeff states. "I heard things haven't been going well for you on the pitch."

"Nah, not sure I want to be a football player anymore," Jack replies glumly, poking at his food.

Jeff nearly chokes on his potato. "*What?* What are you talking about? You love football. Every time we talk, you don't shut up about it."

"I know, but football is supposed to be a team game," Jack snaps. "If you can't trust your team, what's the point? You can never win."

"And why wouldn't you be able to trust your team? You and the team have been doing well. You haven't been at your best in the last few games. There's still time to turn it around, you know," Jeff says encouragingly. "Is this something to do with Tommy? I notice you two have seemed off with each other."

"I don't want to talk about that liar!" Jack blurts out.

The people at the next table take notice.

Jeff leans in closer. "Hey, Jack, I heard what happened," he says quietly.

"Really? How?"

"Oh, I have my sources. I've been here a while, Jack. I've seen it all."

"So you saw how much of a liar he is then," Jack growls.

"I saw that he made a mistake," Jeff responds.

"A pretty *big* mistake!" Jack snaps.

"Maybe, but sometimes people do stupid things," Jeff says calmly. "Sometimes there might be reasons why they do these things, you know?"

"I don't care."

Jeff sits up straight, his voice turns serious. "Well, maybe you should, Jack. I watched you both together on the pitch and off it. There's something special about your relationship. You make each other better. You make each other happier."

"So what? He should have thought about that before spying on me," Jack complains.

Jeff pauses, takes a sip of his ice-cold orange juice, narrows his eyes, and glances around the now half-empty cafeteria to make sure no one is watching. "I'll tell you what, Jack. Why don't you go and visit your old friends, the Bandits? Have some fun for a couple of hours. Get you out of this academy. Don't worry, I'll cover for you. It might do you some good to be with your friends."

"Really?" Jack replies, almost falling off his chair. "I didn't think I would get a chance to see them again."

"Well, here's your chance," Jeff says, smiling. "Let's finish our lunch, get your boots, then get out of here. Maybe they can help you."

"Thanks, Jeff."

"Now finish up, and let's get going."

Jack is excited at the prospect of meeting the Bandits again. It has been months since he's seen them, having had to stay away after the boots fiasco. He's looking forward to being around friends again. Listening to Ryan's bad jokes, which are so terrible, they're funny. Watching Ben and Joe squabble. Seeing Kiera's impressive catalogue of football skills. He can't wait.

18

Truth at The Rec

"The truth is like a good striker -
it always finds its target."

Thierry Henry

As Jack turns onto the pitch, he never thought this day would come. He's meeting the Bandits after almost four months. Excitement courses through his body, making his hands tremble slightly. He arrives at the Rec. Sure enough, there they are.

"Hey, guys, guess who's back!" Jack shouts towards the Bandits, playing at the top of the field.

They all stop, frozen in place like statues.

"Jack?" Kiera responds, squinting her eyes. "Is that...?"

"Yep, it's me," Jack shouts, a grin spreading across his face as wide as a football goal.

They all charge towards him like a pack of excited puppies, stopping just in time to avoid bowling him over.

"What are you doing here? I thought we'd gotten rid of you!" Ryan jokes.

"Yeah, nice to see you, mate," Ben and Joe say in an eerily perfect unison.

"It's good to see you, Jack," Kiera says, her smile as bright as a floodlight.

"It's good to see you guys too. Actually, it's better than good. It's amazing!" Jack exclaims, feeling like he might explode with happiness.

"I know. We're pretty amazing." Ryan smirks, puffing out his chest like a proud rooster.

"Don't mean to be rude, mate, but why are you here?" Kiera asks, her head tilted to one side like a curious puppy.

Jack sighs, his shoulders drooping slightly. "It's a long story. Let's go sit on the bench."

"Race you to it!" Ben jokes, taking off like a rocket.

They all race after him, their feet pounding against the puffy green grass. Soon enough, they reach the park bench, panting and laughing.

"So come on then, spill the beans," Ryan barks, leaning in eagerly.

"Well, something bad has happened. Like, really bad," Jack begins, bowing his head.

"Go on..." Ben prompts.

"So when I first moved to the academy, I met a kid named Tommy before I even knew you guys. We actually got on super well. He was my best friend."

"Hey, that's not allowed! We're your only best friends," Ryan jokes, trying to lighten the mood.

Jack smiles briefly before his face grows serious again. "Well, he did something. Something terrible..."

"Hold on, are you talking about your shoes?" Kiera remarks, raising her eyebrows before jerking her head back slightly. "About them being nicked?"

"Whoa! Are you psychic?" Jack exclaims, blinking rapidly, gazing at Kiera in wonder.

The Bandits all look at each other like they share a secret Jack doesn't know.

"He told us," Joe said quietly, speaking up for the first time.

"Told you what? You met him?" Jack asks, confusion written all over his face.

"Well, duh! Where did you think your new boots came from?" Kiera laughs.

"I assumed you found out from Jeff. That maybe you visited the academy, and he told you," Jack remarks, his mind whirling like a tornado.

"We don't go near that place after they rejected us!" Ryan grumbles.

"Jeff got the boots from us. Tommy organized it," Kiera explains gently.

"I am so confused," Jack replies, rubbing his forehead as if trying to understand everything.

"Maybe we should explain," Kiera continues, her voice patient. She takes a deep breath, her eyes serious. "One day, we were playing Wembley when we noticed a kid watching us from the park. We told him to go away, of course. But he didn't."

"I even tried to scare him away, but he didn't budge," Ryan chips in.

"We asked him what he wanted, and he said he was your friend," Kiera continues.

Eager to hear more, Jack moves closer to Kiera.

"He told us everything. What he had done. Telling some kid called Wilson about what you were doing and stuff."

Jack nods gently, his shoulders tense.

"At first, we were super annoyed," Kiera admits.

"I wanted to tie him to the tree," Ryan jokes, though his eyes showed he was only half-kidding.

"But then we saw how sad he was. Like, super sad. He started crying and everything," Ben adds, gesturing with his hands.

"Anyway, after he stopped crying, he told us other things, too," Kiera says, her tone growing more serious.

"What other things?" Jack asks leaning closer.

"He told us about Wilson. About how every day Wilson bullies him and has done so since the day he arrived."

"No, no, no. I see them talking all the time," Jack protests, shaking his head.

"Did he look happy when they were talking?" Kiera inquires gently.

Jack goes quiet for a moment. His face scrunches up as he thinks hard about what he's seen. Whenever he sees Wilson and Tommy together, Tommy doesn't looked happy. In fact, he looks a little scared.

"Um, not really," Jack replies after a long reflection.

"Exactly!" Kiera exclaims. "Wilson told him that if he didn't spy on you, he would try and get Tommy thrown out of the academy instead."

Jack gasps in surprise.

"Tommy's dad would kill him if that happened. He didn't know what to do. At first, he agreed; he was scared. But then he started to really like you. After you had your boots stolen, he saw how upset you were. He felt super guilty." Kiera pauses, letting her words sink in. "He hated seeing you that upset. Tommy couldn't bear it. Especially after he told Wilson. So, he decided to come up with a plan. A plan that meant he could keep you happy and Wilson off his back."

Jack listens intently, his previous anger slowly melting away as he begins to understand the whole story. "So the whole idea was his?" Jack asks, tilting his head to one side.

"Yep. Jack, he's actually pretty cool. He played with us for a bit after. He's a good mate." Kiera's face turns serious. She looks past Jack, like she's watching an old movie in her head. "Tommy didn't mean to be mean. I bet he felt like he had no choice."

She takes a deep breath. "I know what it feels like. I've been bullied too. It's super scary. When someone's always picking on you, you might do crazy things just to make it stop. Even if you know it's wrong."

"Yeah, I had to give all of my pocket money to one," Ben chips in, his face scrunching up at the memory.

"But...how can I trust him again?" Jack asks, crossing his arms.

"Tommy took a big chance to come see us. He spent his savings and all his pocket money to buy you new boots. He even stopped telling Wilson stuff, even though he knew he might get hurt or kicked out of the academy for it."

"That's a true friend, Jack," Kiera states firmly.

"Yeah, everyone makes mistakes, Jack," Joe adds with a subtle nod.

"It's not what they do that matters. It's what they do after. How they make it up to you," Ben comments, standing with his hands on his hips.

Jack pauses, gazing out at the green field before him. The scent of freshly cut grass fills his nostrils as a soft breeze gently brushes across his face. Rubbing the back of his neck, he lowers his chin to his chest. "Maybe you guys are right."

"Of course, we are right. We're always right," Ryan jokes.

"I feel so bad. I didn't know he was being bullied. I've been so mean to him since I found out."

"You didn't know, Jack. But now you do. It's what you do next that matters," Kiera urges with a slight smile.

"You're right. I'll find a way to make it up to him."

"Well, you better start doing it soon. Don't you have to be back now?"

Jack looks at his watch. His eyebrows shoot towards his hairline. "Yikes. I've been here almost two hours. I need to go, guys. I don't know what to say."

"*Thank you.* That would be nice." Ryan smirks.

"Thank you, guys. Thank you for everything. I will never forget you," Jack sniffles, trying not to cry.

Ben gives Jack a playful punch on the arm. "Cheer up! Who knows what the future holds? We might be teammates one day!"

Joe nods in agreement.

"Yeah, told you, Jack, be a star, buy a mansion, then we can all live in it," Ryan teases.

"Take care of yourself, Jack. Go follow your dreams," Kiera insists, pointing to the gate.

Jack takes a deep breath and looks at his friends one last time. "Bye, everyone," he whispers, his voice strong even though his heart feels heavy.

He waves to the Bandits, trying to remember every detail of their faces. Then, he spins around and starts running. It's time to make amends.

19

The Penalty

"Pressure is just an illusion.
What matters is how you handle it."

Harry Kane

Jack's heart pounds as he places the ball on the penalty spot. The roar of the Kingsdown Academy crowd fades to a distant hum. This is it—the moment that will decide everything. Ten months of blood, sweat, and tears have led to this.

As he takes five steps back, Jack can't help but think about how different things were just a year ago. He was just a ten-year-old kid from Austin, Texas, with a crazy dream, and now here he stands, about to take the most important shot of his life.

The referee's whistle cuts through the air. Jack takes a deep breath, runs forward, and…

Jack stops.

The crowd falls silent, exchanging confused glances. It's game thirty-seven of thirty-eight. Kingsdown is in fourth place, with third place just two points ahead. They needed to win both their remaining games to even stand a chance of finishing third.

Jack returned from his meeting with the Bandits the night before. He initially tried to find Tommy but couldn't. That was when Jack devised a plan to make things right between them.

Throughout the second half of the season, Jack and Tommy were unstoppable together—Tommy, the assister, and Jack, the scorer. Both were happy with the partnership, but Tommy hadn't actually scored a goal all season. Since the fallout, he hadn't even registered an assist. Tommy always told Jack he wasn't bothered about the goals. But there was one person close to him who was—his dad. His dad has always wanted him to be a striker. Tommy loves midfield. He prefers setting up the goals. He likes the comfort of midfield. Being a forward is a high-pressure position, especially the number nine.

This is the last home game of the season. If you play in the academy, you can be sure every parent would be there to watch. Jack knows this could be the perfect moment for Tommy to make his dad proud, something he has always strived to do. News had come in that the team above them had won. This meant there is now a five-point gap. Kingsdown would no longer be the oldest academy in the world if they draw or lose. They'd be an academy no more.

This penalty is vital with the club at stake, ninety minutes on the clock, and the score at zero-zero. For the club, it is a matter of life and death. For Jack, it is his chance to make amends.

The referee's whistle cuts through the air again. Jack takes a deep breath, runs forward, and…

Jack stops.

In an instant, Jack turns to the referee and whispers something to him. Confusion ripples through the stadium like a tidal wave. Time stops. After his brief chat, Jack slowly walks towards his team, and then suddenly, to Tommy's surprise, towards him.

"I want you to take it," Jack states, passing him the ball.

"Eh? You want me to take it? I know you don't like me, but making me miss in front of the whole crowd and my dad? That's your revenge?" Tommy mutters, dropping his head to the floor, his voice a mix of confusion and hurt.

"The Bandits told me everything. Truth is, I'm sorry too, Tommy. I'm not giving you this penalty because I think you'll miss it. I'm giving it to you because I know you'll score," he says, patting him on the back with a massive smile across his face.

"Really?" Tommy murmurs, biting his lip and tapping his fingers on his thigh as he glances around the carnival atmosphere in the stadium.

"Yeah, I've seen how well you take them when we practice. Plus, your dad's here. You can make him proud. Show Wilson how strong you really are," Jack urges with a cheeky grin. "I believe in you, Tommy. Now get out there, make me, your dad, and the crowd proud, and smash that ball into the back of the net!"

Tommy looks at Jack, then into the stands. He hears the chant echo across the stadium: "Kingsdown! Kingsdown! Kingsdown!"

Goosebumps cover Tommy's arms like a prickly sweater. Tommy puts out his hand to Jack, but Jack surprises him, embracing him with a hug.

Pulling Tommy close, he whispers, "You can do it."

Tommy walks towards the ball.

The crowd gasps in shock.

Even the goalkeeper looks confused, shifting from foot to foot like he's standing on hot coals.

Tommy approaches the ball. Resetting it on the penalty spot. He takes five steps back and closes his eyes, imagining the ball crashing into the back of the net, the crowd going wild, and his dad finally being proud of the footballer he's becoming. He takes a deep breath. Clenches his fists.

Then, in the flash of an eye, Tommy runs and strikes the ball with pure power. It flies through the air like a bullet.

Crashes against the right post. Then the left. Then the stadium goes silent.

"GOAL!" the commentators scream, their voices cracking with excitement.

The ball rebounds off the left post and crosses over the line.

The goalie doesn't move, frozen like a statue. The final whistle is blown.

His teammates storm towards him like a herd of excited elephants. Jack stays back and watches as the team lifts Tommy up high, celebrating like they've won the World Cup.

The crowd is ecstatic. Tommy's name echoes across the ground like a battle cry.

Tommy stares up to see his dad. For the first time, he's smiling at something Tommy has done, looking proud. Tommy feels on top of the world, like he can touch the clouds.

Although Kingsdown still hasn't secured their future, they're still in it. Jack's selflessness and Tommy's heroics ensure Kingsdown still has a chance to survive heading into the last game of the season. They are still two points behind, but their destiny is now in their hands.

Next week, they would play their last game of the season. Their opponent? An away game to fourth place Wrexham Warriors.

Anything other than a win, and the club would close. But after today's result, they suddenly believe that maybe the impossible is possible after all. They just need to believe.

Jack is proud of Tommy. For overcoming his fear, scoring his first-ever goal, and making his dad proud. Jack's hatred and anger towards Tommy has vanished into thin air and been replaced with happiness and joy. It feels good to do something nice for somebody else. Hate got him nowhere; forgiveness has changed everything. It has made not just Jack happy but Tommy, his dad, the team, and the entire stadium, too.

Everyone is happy. It's perfect.

Well, almost perfect.

There is one player who doesn't look happy. One player who has always hated Jack.

Jack knows what he has to do. If he's going to save the club and become a star, he has no choice but to overcome his biggest challenge.

Wilson.

20

A New Game Plan

"Sometimes the best plan is to
forget the plan and just play with your heart."

Luis Suárez

It's the last week of a long, gruelling season at the academy. The air buzzes with excitement after their latest win. Hope floats through the academy like a sweet scent.

By now, all the players have heard about the club's situation. They know they won't have a team to play for next year if they don't win their last game of the season. It's like a ticking time bomb, counting down to their final match.

Knowing the importance of their final game on Saturday, Coach Wilkinson insists that all players carry out extra training, just as Jack and Tommy previously inspired the team to do. Everyone is happy to put in the extra work. It's like they're all superheroes, training to save the world—or at least their beloved academy.

But one player is not happy. In fact, he's as grumpy as a bear woken up from hibernation.

Knock Knock

"Come in" Coach shouts from the other side of the office door.

Wilson enters a small room with a wooden desk positioned in the centre. At the back, a small circular window lets in a glimmer of light, and under it sits a plant that looks like its seen better days. The walls display various awards, including "Manager of the Year" and several cup titles. The atmosphere feels stuffy, and an odd, musky odour lingers in the air, reminiscent of old, sweaty boots.

"Coach, why have we got to do extra training? We didn't have to last season," Wilson moans, his face scrunched up like he's just bitten into a lemon.

"That's right. Last year, we had already won the league by now. That's why. There's no way I'm going to be the coach that got the club closed," Coach states, shaking his head. "Why don't you take some inspiration from Jack? He's the one that gave me the idea for extra training sessions."

"I knew it! That kid can't help keep his nose out of other people's business. He's the reason we're in this position!" Wilson growls, his face bright red.

"What's your problem with him, Wilson?" The coach interjects, frowning as he crosses his arms and shakes his head. "You have never taken a liking to him since the day he arrived."

"I don't like newcomers. They always mess everything up. Things were going perfectly well before he arrived," Wilson grumbles.

"Things can't stay the same forever, Wilson. Are you annoyed because he's taken your place? Competition is important. It's vital not just for the club to improve but also for you as a player! Just because you aren't starting doesn't mean we don't need you. Football is a team game. Teamwork and spirit are the most important things."

"Tell that to my parents!" Wilson snaps, his voice cracking slightly.

"Look, Wilson, why don't you just talk to Jack? You'll find he's actually really nice," Coach suggests gesturing broadly.

"Fat chance of that happening now," Wilson mumbles.

"Why?" asks coach, leaning in to listen.

"It doesn't matter. This is going nowhere. I've gotta go. Catch you later, Coach."

Wilson jumps up to leave, opening the creaky office door. Jack is on the other side. Wilson bursts out of the room, almost knocking Jack over.

Coach spots Jack. "Hey, Jack, can I help?"

Jack pauses, glancing back at Wilson before heading inside. "Hey, Coach. I wanted to ask you something."

"Go on…" The coach tilts his head and sits up straight in his ever-squeaky chair.

Jack takes a deep breath, lifting his chin slightly. "So I've been thinking. During the whole season, we've played with just one striker. But in recent games, I've found it challenging to find space. I'm isolated up there."

An eerie silence fills the room.

"Keep going," the coach urges, leaning forward and quirking an eyebrow.

Jack pauses as he spots a picture on the wall of Coach Wilkinson, last year's Manager of the Year. He wonders if he should really be giving advice on team selection to last year's award winner. "The team we're playing next always lines up with five defenders. That makes it even harder to find space and score," he states, fidgeting with the zipper on his shorts.

"Alright, what do you suggest?" Coach replies, narrowing his eyes, focusing intently on Jack.

"Well, we need to score. So maybe we could play with two strikers?" Jack offers, shuffling his feet from side to side as glances around the room.

Coach raises his eyebrows. "Two strikers?"

Jack pauses, covering his mouth for a moment as he debates his next words. "Yeah, it's me and Wilson," he insists, biting his lip slightly.

Coach pauses for a minute, sipping his coffee as he considers Jack's suggestion like a complex puzzle. He rests his head in his hands and exclaims, "I didn't think you two got along?"

"We don't. Well, we didn't. But maybe this can bring us together. Plus, we need all the help we can get if we're going to win. I'm small and fast. Wilson's big and strong. It's the perfect combination," Jack explains, crossing his arms and lifting his chin slightly. "Like peanut butter and jelly!"

"But Wilson has yet to score since Christmas. That's half the season!" Coach points out, frowning as he turns away slightly, his voice filled with doubt.

Jack nods intently, placing his hands on his hips as he stares directly into the coach's eyes. "Exactly. This is the perfect time to end the goal drought," Jack insists.

Coach pauses again, his eyes fixed on the ground as if the answer is written on the floor. "Okay, Jack, but I must warn you. Wilson isn't your biggest fan." He remarks.

"I know. Leave that to me," Jack declares, crossing his arms confidently. "So, can he play on Saturday?" he tilts his head and asks.

The coach pauses, staring at the ground and then at last year's Manager of the Year award. After a moment of thought, he looks up, a small smile forming on his face. "Okay, Jack. I trust you. He can play," he declares, narrowing his gaze with a confident nod.

"Thank you so much!" Jack exclaims, bouncing on his toes, grinning from ear to ear.

"Now get out of here before I change my mind," Coach teases, shooing Jack away with a playful wave.

"Thanks again, coach!" he shouts as he leaves, slamming the creaky door shut for the last time. Chuffed about getting the result he wants. Jack feels as happy as a kid on Christmas morning.

He successfully completes the first part of his plan. The next part is tricky—he needs Wilson to agree. Although Wilson is eager to play, the idea of teaming up with Jack, instead of competing against him, feels like a step too far—like asking a cat to be best friends with a dog. But Jack is determined to make things right, no matter what.

Jack tries all week to approach him. But Wilson refuses to speak to Jack. He won't even look at him. Whenever Jack gets near, Wilson would walk away or, even worse, threaten Jack. But Jack isn't afraid of Wilson anymore. He knows Wilson is just annoyed. Annoyed Jack has taken his place. If anything, Wilson is afraid of Jack.

The night before the game, Jack is journaling, writing down his thoughts—both good and bad—without any judgment. Suddenly, he has a great idea, like a lightbulb going off in his head. Jack has been writing every night for almost five months. He's getting good at it. It's so good that he decides that if he isn't able to speak to Wilson, maybe he could write to him instead.

That night, Jack writes the letter, asking Wilson not to play for Jack but for the club. For his future. Jack's contract finishes at the end of the season. There is no guarantee he would be offered a new one. But Wilson still has two more years on his.

A contract is no good if there's no club to play for. Jack tells him he wants to save the club and is willing to forget everything that happened. To start with a clean slate. He slips it under Wilson's door and leaves it up to fate to decide what happens next.

All Jack can do is hope and pray that he has done enough. If he hasn't, then it would surely spell an end for both Jack's career and the academy itself.

21

The Big Game

"Wearing the number 9 isn't just
about scoring goals, it's about carrying dreams."

Marco van Basten

I t's Saturday. The day of the big game has finally arrived.

Nine months of blood, sweat, and tears have boiled down to this moment. It feels like the world is holding its breath, waiting to see what would happen. An away visit to third place. The stakes couldn't be higher if they tried. The opposition knows a draw would be enough to secure a third spot. They had a safety net, but Kingsdown is walking a tightrope.

Jack has been waiting to hear from Wilson since he slid the letter under his door but has heard only silence. He begins to worry his mission has failed.

The old brick stadium stands proudly at the end of the street. Through the bus windows, hundreds of fans in red scarves head surge toward the large metal gates. The aroma of hot dogs and burgers fills the air as crowds sing their team songs. He presses his hands against the cold glass and spots the giant team badge above the entrance. The enticing smell of hot chocolate and snacks from the stands outside makes his mouth water—they're finally here.

"Hey, mate, don't worry so much," Tommy urges as the bus pulls into the Wrexham Warriors stadium.

"I can't believe you're being so nice to him anyway after what he did. He doesn't deserve to play," Tommy adds, his voice tinged with disbelief.

"Everyone deserves a second chance. Even Wilson," Jack replies. "Plus, it's not about me. We need to save the club, remember?"

"Yeah, maybe you're right. I don't like bullies, you know." Tommy sighs, his shoulders slumping slightly.

"I know, but remember, everyone has their reasons."

They get off the bus and head to the changing rooms. The atmosphere is so tense you could cut it with a knife.

Coach Wilkinson gathers the team. "Right, today we're going to try something a little bit different," he says winking at Jack. "As you know, the team we play today only needs a draw. That means they're going to defend for their lives. That also means we need more firepower. So today, Jack and Wilson, you will play up front in the forward position together. Is that okay with you both?"

He looks towards both Jack and Wilson, his eyebrows raised in question.

Jack nods, his heart pounding like a drum. He immediately turns towards Wilson, not knowing what to expect.

Wilson glances at Jack before looking back at the coach. He finally gives a nod.

"Great. Glad to hear everybody's on board," Coach declares, nodding towards the team. "As you're probably all aware, this season hasn't been our best. In fact, it's actually been one of our worst. But that doesn't mean we can't save it."

Coach clenches his fists, his voice grows stronger. "This is one of the world's oldest and most prestigious academies. We only accept the finest of players. Although results haven't gone our way this season, I have no doubt about the ability of all of you guys.

"But today goes beyond your football abilities. Today is a mental battle. A battle between both sides on who wants it more. Who is prepared to leave everything out on the pitch? To give a hundred and ten percent? To fight for your club. To fight for the fans. To fight for your teammates and, most importantly, your family, who have sacrificed so much just for you to be here."

The room falls silent, every player holding onto Coach's words as if their lives depend on them.

"You are the lucky ones. The chosen ones. This is your chance to make them proud. To make me proud. To be proud of yourselves. I'm not asking you to go out there and win. I'm asking you to go out there and give everything you have. To be soldiers for the team. For one another. Battling away no matter what. Never giving up. Never losing hope. Always believing that anything is possible. If you can do that, then we will still be winners no matter what the score. That is something we can all be proud of."

Coach's voice rises. "Now, Kingsdown, let's get out there and show them what we're capable of. Are you ready?"

"Yes!" the team shouts, their voices a bit shaky but growing in confidence.

"That's not good enough. *Are you ready?*" Coach shouts, his voice echoing off the walls.

"*YES!*" the team screams.

"Well, what are you waiting for? Let's go out there and give them the performance of a lifetime!"

Cheers erupt in the changing rooms as the team makes their way out to the pitch. The excitement is electric, crackling in the air around them. For what could be the final time, Kingsdown Academy steps out onto the field, ready to fight for their future.

The game kicks off. The atmosphere is tense, like the calm before a storm. The home crowd is thunderous, their cheers and chants a constant roar. But Kingsdown starts the game well. They immediately pressure the opposition into mistakes, winning the ball back with ease. Hounding the opposition. They're everywhere at once, like a swarm of determined bees.

They have plenty of the ball, but Coach is right. The Wrexham Warriors are defending for their lives. With a back five, opportunities take a lot of work. Kingsdown is limited to back and side passes. Wrexham Warriors has built a wall so big that it would take a tank to break through.

Thirty minutes pass, and although Kingsdown have seventy percent possession, they are still yet to have a shot on target. They just can't work out the combination to the safe.

After another fifteen minutes pass, the referee blows for halftime. With the score at zero-zero and Kingsdown unable to break through the defence, Kingsdown heads into halftime feeling deflated. If they don't do something soon, their beloved team could disappear forever.

22

The Second Half

"It's not how you start,
it's how you finish."

Ian Rush

The team enter the changing rooms. The atmosphere is noticeably sour, like milk left out too long. Coach decides he needs to have a word. His voice cuts through the gloomy silence.

"Gather round, everyone," he says calmly, his eyes scanning the faces of his team. "Now I know the half didn't exactly go how many of you thought it would. But remember, football is a game of two halves. This game is far from over. We need to try and get the ball to Jack and Wilson."

"But it's impossible. There're just so many defenders," Tommy states, shaking his head.

"I know. That's why we need to use more of our superpower," Coach urges.

"Superpower?" Jack responds, his eyebrows furrowing in confusion.

"Teamwork," Coach states, narrowing his eyes. "You are all having excellent individual games. Playing some of the best football I've seen you play. I'm proud. But we need to work as a team. When somebody gets the ball, you need to help them. Find space for them to pass to you. Otherwise, they have little choice but to pass back. I don't care if you lose the ball. I want you to try. To be there for one another. When somebody gets the ball, they should have at least three players they can pass to."

"But then we'll be out of position," Wilson chips in, worry creasing his forehead.

"That's okay," Coach replies, calm and reassuring. "Football is about risk. About doing things you aren't sure of. That's what makes it so exciting. It's high stakes. Decision-making at the top level. I believe in you guys. You just need to believe in one another."

The team nods, their faces set with determination.

"One more thing."

The team listens intently. Leaning in closer.

"Have fun! You guys are so serious out there" — coach declares as he stands with his hands on his hips. Gazing at every player, as he turns to face them in the changing room. — "why did you start playing football in the first place? Because it's fun—that's why! It's exciting! I want you to go out and enjoy your football. To play with creativity, joy and freedom. After all, that's why we love the game, right?" The coach barks as he nods his head and raises his arms.

The team nods in unison.

"Now let's get out there and show them the real Kingsdown Academy!"

The team immediately makes their way out, rejuvenated by Coach Wilkinson's talk. Pumped. Ready to give it their all, no matter what. It's time to show the world what Kingsdown is really made of.

Kingsdown kicks off, the ball rolling across the pitch like the start of an adventure. Immediately, they try to attack. Two race down opposite sides, their feet flying over the grass like they have wings.

Tommy sends the ball down the left, a perfect pass slicing through the air. It reaches Ginger, the winger, who immediately passes to Jack ahead in the penalty box.

Jack manages to turn the defender, twisting like a tornado.

He shoots. But it goes wide, sailing past the goal.

"Well done. Keep going!" Coach roars.

They do, continuously attacking the opposition. Constantly creating space and opportunities for one another, operating like a well-oiled machine. Their one-touch passing so quick, commentators can barely keep up with who has it.

Wrexham Warriors struggle to keep up with the lightning-fast play. Stuck in their own half, like fish trapped in a net.

But yet, with all the pressure, Kingsdown still can't seem to break down the opposition. Their passing is slick. But the shots are forced. Striking the ball from a distance in the false hope that it might somehow find its way in. With no end product, things are looking bad.

Then, with just ten minutes left of the game, something magical happens.

Wrexham has a rare corner—their first of the game.

Most of Kingsdown rush back to defend, but Coach tells Wilson and Jack to stay put. Hovering around the centre circle.

A risky move. A gamble.

If Wrexham score, there's surely no way back for Kingsdown. But Coach always says football is about risk. About taking chances. This is their chance.

The referee blows his whistle.

The Wrexham midfielder swings the corner in, arcing through the air like a boomerang.

But it doesn't beat the first man. The defence immediately heads it out. The ball flies through the air. Eventually finding its way to Tommy, who takes one look up, scanning the field like a hawk, before instantly playing a through ball forward towards Jack.

A pass so perfect, it's like Tommy could see the future.

Jack manages to get on the end of it and bursts down the left wing. He moves so fast that he's just a blur of colour.

Wrexham are scrambling to get back, most of their team still in the Kingsdown penalty box, completely out of position.

Jack is fast—faster than fast. He approaches the last third of the pitch. With only one player ahead of him, he spots an opportunity. He decides to use his pace, knocking the ball forward twenty yards, then sprinting like his life depends on it.

He's like a rocket. Passing the last defender with ease, leaving him in his dust.

On the edge of the box with only the goalie in his sights, he knows exactly where he wants to shoot. An almost certain goal. The crowd roars in anticipation.

Out the corner of his eye, Jack spots Wilson by the far post, completely unmarked. Waving his arms like a windmill, calling for the ball.

Jack takes another touch to the left, drawing the keeper towards him, before calmly rolling the ball back into the middle.

Past the charging keeper. Reaching Wilson.

Wilson takes a touch.

BOOM!

Wilson smashes it past the confused keeper, who was convinced Jack would shoot for himself.

The ball hits the back of the net. The stadium explodes. The away fans erupt in celebration, their cheers shaking the stadium. Teammates swarm Wilson, high-fiving in unison. Coach Wilkson runs down the touchline to congratulate him too.

The referee blows his whistle to calm things down. The game isn't over yet.

As they head back to the centre circle, Wilson approaches a surprised Jack with the biggest grin Jack has ever seen.

"Hey, thanks, mate. Great pass," Wilson says, his voice filled with genuine gratitude.

"No problem. Great finish," Jack replies, smiling back.

"Now let's finish the job!"

With Kingsdown one-zero up, they have to do precisely what Wrexham has been doing the whole game—defend.

And defend they do. They defend like their lives depend on it, blocking every shot, cutting out every pass and winning every header. They have come this far. None of the players are prepared to let it slip away now.

Then, after ten gruelling minutes of non-stop defending, where every second feels like an hour, the referee finally blows his whistle. It's music to their ears. Kingsdown has won one-zero!

Victory crashes over them like a tidal wave, sweeping away months of doubt, fear, and pressure. Some players collapse to their knees, their legs finally acknowledging just how tired they are. Jack tastes salt—whether from sweat, tears, or both, he isn't sure. The future they fight for, dream about, and lose sleep over becomes a solid reality, as real as the grass beneath their boots and the teammates by their side. This isn't just a win; it's their legacy at Kingsdown, carved into history.

The celebration erupts across the pitch. Players leap, spin, and collide in a euphoric dance of triumph. Zico lifts Tommy onto his shoulders. The usually stern Coach Wilkinson abandons his clipboard, swept up in the tide of emotion. The away fans transform their corner of the stadium into a carnival, their songs rolling across the pitch in waves. Red and white scarves whip through the air like victory flags, each chant growing louder than the last, until the very ground pulses with their energy.

At the touchline, the owner collapses into Coach's embrace. Decades of tradition and future dreams collide in that single moment. Their usual professional distance dissolves as Coach's shoulders shake with relief, while the owner repeatedly whispers, "Thank you, thank you," into the evening air. Kingsdown Academy, the grand old lady of English football, would live to see another day.

22

Rivals To Friends

"In my career, I learned that sometimes your greatest rival is actually the person who will push you to become your best self. And when rivalry turns to friendship, that's when real magic happens."

Luis Suárez

NUMBER 9: THE BEGINNING | Jack Scorer

As most of the team is celebrating, Jack stands at the centre circle. Every sight and sound demand his attention: the worn spot where the referee always stands for penalties, the squeak of the rusty goal frame that makes saves feel more dramatic, and the exact shade of green that the groundskeeper meticulously cares for. His mind fills like a photo album, capturing not just images but feelings—the pride of wearing the jersey, the thrill of hearing his name chanted, and the familiar muscle ache after training. Some people say it's just a game, a field, and a school. But standing here now, Jack knows better; it's where he discovers who he can become.

As he's absorbing the atmosphere, somebody taps him on the back. It's Wilson. Before Jack can say a word, Wilson embraces him in a bear hug, nearly squeezing all the air out of him.

"Thank you so much, mate. That goal you gave me means a lot to my family and me. I owe you one," Wilson insists, his voice thick with emotion.

"No, thank you for such an amazing finish. It was awesome!" Jack replies, grinning from ear to ear.

"Couldn't have done it without your pinpoint pass," Wilson jokes. Wilson then lowers his head, his face suddenly serious. "Hey, Jack, I know I haven't exactly been very nice to you since you arrived…."

Jack cuts him off, smiling, "It's okay. I get it. I was the new kid. We both play number nine. I took your position. I would be annoyed too!"

"You would?" Wilson yelps.

"For sure! I probably wouldn't have gone as far as paying some local thugs to take my boots though! That was pretty clever," Jack jokes, smiling.

Wilson looks to the ground, shuffling his feet, a little embarrassed. "Yeah, I think I kinda got a little carried away. I watch way too many movies!"

"It's okay. Water under the bridge," Jack responds placing his hand on Wilsons shoulder. He turns to walk away.

"You were right by the way! What you said before when I told you about Tommy. I was scared of you."

"Scared of me? You're twice my size!" Jack jokes, trying to lighten the mood.

"Well, you kind of remind me of my little brother," Wilson states softly. "You see, I'm the oldest. At first, I'm the favorite son. I excel at everything for years. My dad takes me everywhere—football games, movies, the park. Wherever he goes, I follow. But then my brother suddenly starts improving, and everything changes. Instantly, he becomes the center of attention—everyone adores him as the golden boy, the smart one. I know it's selfish of me to want all the attention, even with both of us around. It just feels like he's good at everything: spelling, math, drawing, and, worst of all, football. My dad always seems frustrated with me, asking why I can't be more like my brother. I grow angrier and angrier, and that's why I take my anger out on other people, like Tommy and you."

Jack raises his eyebrows and leans in to listen closer. Noticing a softer tone to Wilson's voice.

"But then I found Kingsdown. They loved me. I was the main boy again. The golden boy. The star player. It was all going so well. Wilson pauses, dropping his chin to his chest and fidgeting with the string on his shorts.

But then you turned up, and it all began to change. At the start it was ok. You know you weren't that good, like my brother you know?" – quirking an eyebrow and cracking a smile towards Jack - "But then you got better and better. I was just scared that I would become invisible again, that's all. I messed up. I'm really sorry. I didn't mean to hurt you or Tommy." He insists bowing his head.

Jack smiles, leaning back slightly, "Hey, it's okay. You apologized. You made things right. That's what really matters," he insists, patting Wilson on the shoulder. "By the way, I'm sure your parents love you both the same. Parents can be weird sometimes. But at the end of the day, they'll always love us. Luckily, I don't think they have a choice," he teases, cocking his head to the side.

Wilson lifts his chin, as a big smile cracks across his face like the sun breaking through the clouds. "Well, thanks anyway, mate. For understanding. It means a lot. Who knows, next year we might be playing alongside each other every game. How cool would that be?"

"That would be awesome!" Jack agrees, nodding his head uncontrollably.

"Well, I'm going to join the celebrations now. Want to come?" Wilson asks, gesturing towards their cheering teammates.

Jack pauses, gazing at Zico and Tommy waving their hands up and down towards the crowd to an array of cheers. "I will. I'm just going to stay here a little longer, soak it all in," Jack replies, leaning back, still marvelling at the day's events.

"Okay, catch you in a bit," Wilson says, jogging off to join the others.

Jack stands there, letting the sounds and sights of victory wash over him. Wilson's words mean a lot. But it's his last words that really stick in Jack's mind. Would they play together next season? Or would this be the last professional youth game of Jack's career?

Jack is desperate to be a star. But for the first time in his life, he isn't worried about it. He wants to celebrate with his team. Let whatever is about to happen, happen.

23

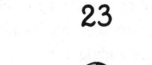

The Meeting

"Sometimes the most important victories happen off the pitch."

Diego Milito

Twenty-four hours have passed since the heroics of the team. Many academy players are beginning to pack up for summer vacation, safe in the knowledge that the club would be here next season.

Jack and Tommy are deep in conversation about yesterday's game drama when the crackly loudspeaker interrupts them.

"Can Jack Scorer please come to the manager's office? Thank you."

Butterflies swirl in Jack's stomach. This is it. The moment he has been waiting for.

"You'll be fine. Why wouldn't they want you?" Tommy jokes.

Jack smiles. Making his way down the twisty hallway, he eventually arrives at the office. Pacing up and down. He begins to sweat. His heart feels like it's going to explode. *Knock-knock!*

"Come in, Jack."

Jack enters the musky office. He freezes. Not just Coach, but the owner too! Something big must be happening - the owner never shows up for player meetings.

"Please have a seat," Coach suggests, gesturing towards the old wooden chair beneath his desk. Coach smiles, leans back in his chair, and begins, "So, Jack, what a journey it has been."

Jack nods.

"You arrive as a shy little boy, and now look at you, leading the team to glory on the last day of the season," he says, pointing a finger at Jack, a slight smile spreading across his face.

"It wasn't just me," Jack remarks, trying to wipe his sweaty palms on his shorts without being noticed.

"Modest too, it seems," the owner chips in, gesturing broadly towards jack with a rare grin.

Then the room falls silent. He hears only the tick-tock of the clock and the rain tapping on the window like tiny fingers. Jack is grateful, worrying that without these sounds, they would hear his heart pounding out of his chest instead.

Coach shuffles some papers on his desk and takes a sip of coffee. "Now, Jack, you are one of our best players at this academy. Your passion, determination, and spirit are incredible. None of us expect such talent from a competition winner. However, as you know, the rule of the competition states that your contract lasts only one season." He refocuses his narrow eyes on Jack.

Jack smiles, leaning in closer.

"Well, you know we have been very impressed with you. Your transformation since last year has been remarkable." Coach declares nodding his head in amazement.

Jack nods, lifting his chin up slightly.

"You also know that the club hasn't been doing well. In fact, without that win yesterday, the club would have no money left." He murmurs, raising his eyebrows.

Jack nods again.

Coach glances around the room at the awards and trophies scattered about. "Finishing first, as usual, means we get a significant amount of prize money. We use this money to sign new players or renew contracts. But this year, Jack, we don't receive that money," he whispers, rolling his eyes as a frown begins to form on his weathered face.

Jack rubs the back of his sweat-soaked neck, a confused expression crossing his face.

The coach pauses, glancing down at the floor for a moment before focusing intently on Jack, his lips pressed tightly together. "Unfortunately, Jack, as much as we want to sign you, we just don't have the funds, especially for an international player," he says, his voice trembling slightly.

Jack's head drops. A tear falls down his cheek.

The owner puts his hand softly on Jacks shoulder, lowering his voice. "But Jack, I want you to know how grateful I am from the bottom of my heart. Without you, my beloved club would have had to close. My dad gave this club to me, and it would have broken my heart if I had lost it. So thank you." He whispers, bowing his head.

"He's right," the coach agrees, placing a reassuring hand on Jack's opposite shoulder. "You did everything right. It's not your fault; that's just how life is sometimes. I believe you have a bright future ahead of you. If you don't become a star here, you will shine somewhere else. I know it." He declares proudly, nodding his head.

"Thanks," Jack whispers, jerking his head back slightly, wiping the lone tear from his face.

"Who knows, maybe our paths cross again in the future," the owner says, lifting his hands enthusiastically in the air to lighten the mood.

Jack rocks his head forward and gets up from his chair. "Well thank you for letting me play here. It's the best experience I've ever had—truly awesome!" he declares, a smile replacing his frown.

The coach smiles and places his hands on his hips. "Hey! We're happy to have you here! As we say, I have a feeling we'll meet again someday. So don't think of this as a goodbye, but rather as a temporary farewell," he jokes, playfully pointing his finger at Jack.

"We have arranged a taxi to take you to the airport. It will arrive in a few hours. So go and say your goodbyes," the owner urges, smiling, trying to hide his sadness.

Jack pauses, scans the room for one last time, before giving a reassuring nod to both coach and owner. "I will. Thanks again. For everything."

Jack leaves feeling a little deflated. Making his way back to his dorm down the winding corridor for the final time, he arrives and opens the door.

"How did it go?" Tommy barks like an excited dog, momentarily startling Jack.

Jack takes a seat on his bed, turning away slightly. "Erm, not how I thought."

Tommy sits next to him, raising an eyebrow. "What do you mean? Are they going to sign you?" he exclaims, shaking the bed with excitement.

Jack looks down at the floor, kicking a stray sock. "They want to sign me, but because the club doesn't have the money, they can't," he whispers softly, his eyes fixed on the ground.

Tommy jumps up, blinking rapidly. "What? That's awful!" he shouts, almost deafening Jack..

"I know. But at least they wanted to. I guess that's what matters," Jack murmurs, dropping his shoulders.

"So sorry mate! That sucks! When do you leave?"

"The taxi will arrive in about three hours," Jack replies reluctantly, finally looking up.

"Wow, that's fast. Damn. I was really looking forward to playing with you next year, mate!" Tommy declares slamming his fist on the bed.

"Me too. But who knows, maybe we will meet again in the future," Jack replies raising his arms with a soft smile.

We can still keep in contact, right?" Tommy urges, putting out his hand for a routine high-five.

"Of course. You're my best friend. I just don't have a contract!" Jack jokes, slamming his hand into Tommy's with a satisfying thud.

The two then begin to pack away their things, talking about the games they played, the goals they scored, and the fun they had. Jack feels sad that he's leaving, but he's happy knowing that he has made a friend, a best friend—something that can't be taken from him.

A few hours pass, and soon enough, the taxi arrives. Jack takes in the sights and sounds of the academy for one last time, before making his way to the exit. He says his goodbyes to Tommy, Zico, Wilson, and all his teammates, wishing them well for the next season. He hugs Jeff and thanks him for all the advice and help he has given him throughout his stay. Jack thanks Coach and the owner for the opportunity before, finally, it's time to leave.

He climbs into the jet-black taxi, tearfully waving goodbye to everyone for the final time. Everyone comes out to wish him good luck.

The taxi pulls away and leaves Kingsdown Academy in its dust. Jack is a little sad, not only because he won't play for Kingsdown again but also because of the friends he's leaving behind: his best friend Tommy, Zico, the Bandits, and even Wilson.

Although down, he's also grateful, grateful for the whole experience, grateful to play at the top level, to have learnt so much, and to have improved both as a person and as a player. He feels more confident, more assured. He's no longer the shy little boy from before, but a confident young man.

He's also proud—proud of himself, proud that he gave it his all. He is proud of helping his teammates. He is proud of saving the club and, most of all, proud that he did it all by himself, away from home, against all odds. No matter what came his way, he overcame it. He knows whatever he puts his mind to, he can achieve.

He's done it. Whether he's signed or not, Jack still feels like a star.

24

Mr. Banks'
Offer of a Lifetime

"When opportunity knocks,
make sure you're ready to open the door."

Filippo Inzaghi

As Jack takes in the sights of London for the final time, the taxi finally arrives at the airport. He doesn't want it to end. It has been so much fun, but he's looking forward to seeing his family and friends back in the States. It has been almost a year! Jack thanks the driver and makes his way towards the airport entrance.

As Jack opens the sliding doors, cool air hits his face immediately. Suitcases bump across the floor, and voices echo off the tall ceiling. The smell of coffee and doughnuts wafts from the small shops. Everyone hurries around as if they are about to miss their flights.

As he makes his way toward the check-in desk, he suddenly hears something in the distance. It sounds like his name. He tries to ignore it, but the voice grows louder until, suddenly, something taps him on the back.

Jack jumps in surprise.

"Sorry to scare you, Jack" — Instantly a tall man appears in front of Jack. Dressed in a black tuxedo equipped with a top hat and the shiniest shoes Jack had ever seen. He also had one of the biggest Mustaches he had ever seen too — "My name is Mr Banks." The man confidently declares.

Jack begins to fidget with his trouser pocket. "Umm, okay, I shouldn't really speak to strangers. Plus, I have a flight to catch." Jack states, turning his head to move forward, ignoring the stranger.

"I'm a friend of the Bandits!" the man blurts out in desperation.

Jack stops and turns. "How do you know about the Bandits?" he asks, narrowing his eyes curiously.

The man smiles and pauses for a moment to straighten his top hat before kneeling to Jack's level. "Well, I own the old supermarket. You play there with your friends, always kicking the ball against the wall," he jokes playfully.

Jack's face turns pale, his palms become sweaty, and he begins to shake.

"Don't look so worried, You're not in trouble. In fact, it's the opposite," the man whispers patting Jack softly on the shoulder.

Jack leans back, his shoulders relax a little.

"I watched you. You and your friends play there every day. It brought me such joy. I have always loved football. Ever since I was young, I wanted to be a football player. But my dad was a businessman. He wanted me to take over his business, so I never got the chance to play. My dad owned the supermarket you played at. He owned a lot of supermarkets—fifty, to be precise." He declares, lifting his chin slightly.

"Okay..." Jack responds, tilting his head and glancing at the departures screen behind the man, worried he might miss his flight.

"Well, my dad passed away recently. It makes me realize just how short life is. Like I said, I love football. But I'm a little old to play now, but it got me thinking. I love watching you guys play. You play with such joy and passion. I see such great talent in all of you. I just don't want it to go to waste. That's when I made my decision," he exclaims.

Jack raises an eyebrow. "What decision?" he inquires, tilting his head again in curiosity.

The man stands with his hands proudly on his hips. "To sell all the supermarkets and start my own football club!" he declares a bit too loudly, catching the attention of a passersby, who glances over briefly, before hurriedly continuing with their own business.

Jack frowns, blinking rapidly. "Your own football team?"

"Yep," the man replies confidently, nodding his head.

Jack glances at the departures board one more time. "That's pretty cool mister, but I don't understand. What does this have to do with me? I really need to get going," he insists, shifting his weight from side to side.

The smiling man pauses for a moment, then defiantly points his finger at Jack. "I want you to lead it, Jack."

Jack's jaw drops. "Lead it?"

"Yep, I have seen your passion, your determination, your fight. I want my football club to be just that."

"Uh? Is this a joke?" Jack interjects, covering his mouth in disbelief.

The man shakes his head, his wispy moustache glowing under the airport lights. "Far from it, my boy. I have already purchased the land, stadium, equipment and the kit. All I need now are the players!"

Jack pauses, narrowing his eyes, trying to take it all in.

The man frowns. "I can tell you aren't sure. Let me share a few more things with you before you decide."

Jack edges his head forward, raising his eyebrows, intrigued by the man.

"I will pay for your accommodation, all your expenses, including monthly travel for your parents to visit, and I'll even offer you a three-year contract." Mr Banks confidently offers, gesturing broadly.

Jack's awe struck as he pauses to think, glancing around the airport like the answer hides among the million suitcases being wheeled about. But, before he can respond, Mr. Banks interrupts him.

"Oh, and one more thing. You aren't the only player I'm interested in. In fact, I've already signed four others. I think you know them," he teases, a mischievous grin spreading across his face like that of a Cheshire cat.

"Who?" Jack inquires, tilting his head to one side, curiosity getting the better of him.

Mr Banks pauses once more, before leaning forward "Your friends, the Bandits,"

"No way!" Jack gasps. "The Bandits? Kiera, Ryan, Ben, and Joe? They're playing for your team?" Jack bounces on his toes, unable to stand still.

"Yep, they all signed contracts yesterday." He declares crossing his arms and nodding his head.

Jack freezes in awe. Gazing into the distance, imagining what it would be like to play professionally with his best friends at a brand-new club, where he will get to be captain. It sounds too good to be true.

"What's the catch?" Jack asks, raising his eyebrows suspiciously.

"No catch. The only catch is I want you to give everything for your team. Like you did with Kingsdown."

"Wait, how did you know about Kingsdown?" Jack murmurs, a little confused.

"Our supermarket used to sponsor them. I know the owner well. The owner told me they couldn't sign you. So I knew I had to! They told me just how good you were!"

"I couldn't pass up the opportunity, so I hurried here as quickly as I could! — He stares at Jack directly in his eyes — "So, what do you say, Jack? How would you like to become our number nine and lead my club to the top?" he declares, standing up straight, holding out his hand.

Jack pauses.

"Well, I need to ask my parents, but—"

"They already know. I contacted them and have flown them in. They are waiting just around the corner. They wanted it to be a surprise," Mr. Banks interrupted.

Jack almost falls over.

"So, what do you say? Is that a yes?" the owner urges, biting his nails, still nervously holding his hand out in front of jacks.

Jack pauses for a moment, glancing at the departure board, before turning back to Mr. Banks. A huge smile spreads across his face as he slaps his hand against Mr. Banks.

"Let's do it! I'm in!" Jack exclaims as he shakes Mr. Banks's hand.

As they walk away from the busy departure gate, Jack can hardly believe how much his life has changed. A year ago, he was just a boy from Texas with a golden ticket and a dream. Now, he is about to captain a brand-new team with his best friends from the streets of London.

He remembers his dad's words: "It's not about being a star—it's about shining bright enough to help others shine, too."

Gazing at the contract in his hands, Jack realizes this isn't the end of his story.

It's only the beginning.

FOOTBALL SPEAK: YOUR GUIDE TO THE BEAUTIFUL GAME

"The beautiful game is beautiful because anyone can understand it."

Paolo Rossi

BASIC TERMS

Pitch - The football field (not the kind you throw in baseball!)

Boots - Football shoes with special studs on the bottom

Kit - The uniform players wear (shirt, shorts, and socks)

Match - The game itself

Fixture - A scheduled game

Training - Practice sessions

POSITIONS

Striker - The player who scores most of the goals (like Jack!)

Midfielder - Players who help both attack and defend

Defender - Players who stop the other team from scoring

Goalkeeper (or Goalie) - The player who guards the goal

Winger - Fast players who run up and down the sides of the pitch

MOVES & SKILLS

Nutmeg - When you kick the ball through another player's legs (tricky!)

Header - Hitting the ball with your head

Tackle - When you try to take the ball from another player

Dribbling - Running with the ball at your feet (not the basketball kind!)

Through Ball - A pass that goes between defenders

Free Kick - A kick awarded after a foul

Penalty - A free shot at goal from the penalty spot

COOL BRITISH FOOTBALL WORDS

Pitch Perfect - When everything goes right in a game

Man On! - Warning a teammate that an opponent is coming

Get in! – Praise for a good goal

Gaffer - Another word for coach or manager

Hat-trick - When one player scores three goals in a game

Own Goal - Accidentally scoring in your own team's goal (oops!)

Football - Soccer

PLACES

Academy - A special school where young footballers train

Changing Room - Where players get ready

Dugout - Where the coach and substitutes sit during a game

Stadium - Where big matches are played

Training Ground - Where teams practice

GAME SITUATIONS

Offside - You can't be behind the last defender when your teammate passes to you.

Corner Kick - When the ball goes out over the goal line off a defender or goalkeeper

Throw-in - How you restart play when the ball goes out on the side line

Extra Time - Additional minutes added to the end of each half

Injury Time - More minutes added for when players were hurt

SCORING & RESULTS

Score line - The current score of the game

Draw - When both teams have the same score

Victory - Winning the game

Defeat - Losing the game

Clean Sheet - When your team doesn't let in any goals

FUN FOOTBALL SAYINGS

"The Beautiful Game" - A nickname for football

"Football's Coming Home" - A famous English football song

"On Form" - When a player is playing really well

"In Space" - When a player is in a good position with no defenders nearby

"Box to Box" - A player who runs up and down the whole pitch

Hey there, soccer fans!

As an ex-player and lifelong soccer/football fan. I hope you enjoyed reading this story as much as I enjoyed writing it!

Watching our characters tackle challenges and celebrate victories was a blast, and I hope it inspired you to have just as much fun with your own soccer journey.

Remember, every time you play, you're learning and getting better, just like the characters you met here.

So, keep practicing, stay curious, and most importantly— have fun out there on the field!

"Football isn't just a game, it's a way of life."
- Eusebio

Until next time,
Jack Scorer

"**P.S.** I've got a little surprise waiting for you—just scan the code on the next page!"

Love soccer? Join our team!

Scan the code to sign up for our free newsletter and get a **FREE** printable (PDF) soccer coloring book with 40 Short Stories of some of the best soccer players on the planet.

https://kickbooks.ck.page

You will be the first to gain **exclusive** early access to the next book in Jack's journey, where he teams up with the Bandits to create an entirely new soccer team! Plus, **more motivational soccer** stories, **activity books,** and even more **free gifts** coming your way soon. Don't miss out!

Made in the USA
Middletown, DE
20 December 2024

67754451R00109